7.99

✓

Sylvia Plath

Open Guides to Literature

Series Editor: Graham Martin (Professor of Literature, The Open University)

Titles in the Series

Richard Bradford: *Paradise Lost*
Angus Calder: Byron
Jenni Calder: *Animal Farm* and *1984*
Walford Davies: Dylan Thomas
Roger Day: Larkin
Peter Faulkner: Yeats
Anthony Fothergill: *Heart of Darkness*
P.N. Furbank: Pound
Brean Hammond: *Gulliver's Travels*
Graham Holderness: *Hamlet*
Graham Holderness: *Women in Love*
Graham Holderness: *Wuthering Heights*
Jeannette King: *Jane Eyre*
Robyn Marsack: Sylvia Plath
Graham Martin: *Great Expectations*
Pam Morris: *Bleak House*
David B. Pirie: Shelley
Gareth Roberts: *The Faerie Queene*
Robert Shaughnessy: Three Socialist Plays
Jeremy Tambling: Narrative and Ideology
Jeremy Tambling: What is Literary Language?
Ronald Tamplin: Seamus Heaney
Dennis Walder: Ted Hughes
Roderick Watson: MacDiarmid
Ruth Whittaker: *Tristram Shandy*

ROBYN MARSACK

Sylvia Plath

Open University Press
Buckingham · *Philadelphia*

Open University Press
Celtic Court
22 Ballmoor
Buckingham
MK18 1XW

and

1900 Frost Road, Suite 101
Bristol, PA 19007, USA

First Published 1992

British Library Cataloging-in-Publication Data

Marsack, Robyn
  Sylvia Plath. – (Open guides to literature series)
  I. Title II. Series
  821

  ISBN 0-335-09353-1
  ISBN 0-335-09352-3 pbk

Library of Congress Cataloging-in-Publication Data

Marsack, Robyn.
   Sylvia Plath / Robyn Marsack.
     p. cm. – (Open guides to literature)
   Includes bibliographical references and index.
   ISBN 0-335-09352-3 (pbk)   0-335-09353-1
   1. Plath, Sylvia – Criticism and interpretation.   I. Title.
II. Series.
PS3566.L27Z777   1992
811'.54 – dc20   91-31683
                                                            CIP

Typeset by Best-set Typesetter, Hong Kong
Printed in Great Britain by J.W. Arrowsmith, Bristol

'What's art but an intense life?'
                    Henry James, 'The Lesson of the Master'

Contents

Series Editor's Preface

The intention of this series is to provide short introductory books about major writers, texts, and literary concepts for students of courses in Higher Education which substantially or wholly involve the study of Literature.

The series adopts a pedagogic approach and style similar to that of Open University material for Literature courses. *Open Guides* aim to inculcate the reading 'skills' which many introductory books in the field tend, mistakenly, to assume that the reader already possesses. They are, in this sense, 'teacherly' texts, planned and written in a manner which will develop in the reader the confidence to undertake further independent study of the topic. They are 'open' in two senses. First, they offer a three-way tutorial exchange between the writer of the *Guide*, the text or texts in question, and the reader. They invite readers to join in an exploratory discussion of texts, concentrating on their key aspects and on the main problems which readers, coming to the texts for the first time, are likely to encounter. The flow of a *Guide* 'discourse' is established by putting questions for the reader to follow up in a tentative and searching spirit, guided by the writer's comments, but not dominated by an over-arching and single-mindedly-pursued argument or evaluation, which itself requires to be 'read'.

Guides are also 'open' in a second sense. They assume that literary texts are 'plural', that there is no end to interpretation, and that it is for the reader to undertake the pleasurable task of discovering meaning and value in such texts. *Guides* seek to provide, in compact form, such relevant biographical, historical and cultural information as bears upon the reading of the text, and they point the reader to a selection of the best available critical discussions of it. They are not in themselves concerned to propose, or to counter, particular readings of the texts, but rather to put *Guide* readers in a position to do that for themselves. Experienced

travellers learn to dispense with guides, and so it should be for
readers of this series.

    This *Open Guide* is best studied in conjunction with Sylvia
Plath's *Collected Poems*, published by Faber and Faber (London,
1981). Page references in the *Guide* are to this edition.

Graham Martin

Acknowledgements

I am glad to acknowledge here the helpful comments on the draft from Nicola Bradbury and Michael Freeman; the patient guidance of Graham Martin; and the support of Stuart Airlie. I am grateful also to the Scottish Arts Council for a writing bursary. To Nicole Jordan, who made Plath and Lowell such living voices to me, and commented on the draft with her usual mixture of astringency and encouragement, my thanks as always.

The photograph on p. 27 and the draft page of 'The Moon and the Yew Tree' are reproduced courtesy of the Manuscripts Department, Lilly Library, Indiana University (Bloomington, Indiana). The photograph on p. 3 is by Landshoff. It is reproduced courtesy of *Mademoiselle*. Copyright © 1953 (renewed 1981) by The Condé Nast Publications Inc.

1. Introduction: 'Over-exposed, like an X-ray'

In 1936 Professor and Mrs Plath, with their two children, moved house from Boston to Winthrop (Massachusetts), close to the sea and to Mrs Plath's parents at Point Shirley. Sylvia was nearly four, born on 27 October 1932. This early access to a seascape, to the rhythms of the sea, was immensely important to Plath, as she writes in 'Ocean 1212-W', a title taken from her grandmother Schober's telephone number:

> My childhood landscape was not land but the end of the land – the cold, salt, running hills of the Atlantic. I sometimes think my vision of the sea is the clearest thing I own. I pick it up, exile that I am ... and in one wash of memory the colors deepen and gleam, the early world draws breath.
>
> Breath, that is the first thing. Something is breathing. My own breath? The breath of my mother? No, something else, something larger, farther, more sensuous, more weary.... The motherly pulse of the sea made mock of such counterfeits [wind and rain]. Like a deep woman, it hid a good deal: it had many faces, many delicate, terrible veils. It spoke of miracles and distances; if it could court, it could also kill. (*Johnny Panic and the Bible of Dreams*, p. 117)[1]

You will pick up these recurring images in the poems, but you may also like to think about this landscape in comparison to the landscapes which nourish the poems of the younger Auden, or of Dylan Thomas, both poets whom Plath read carefully. Was Elizabeth Hardwick making a useful distinction when she said that Plath's sea imagery was 'not particularly local but rather psychological'?[2]

The seaside childhood continued happily – Mrs Plath describes her daughter as 'a healthy, merry child' in her introduction to *Letters Home*[3] – but increasingly independent from the world of the Plath family. Sylvia's brother, Warren, was not a very healthy child, and when not occupied with him Mrs Plath was attending to her husband. Twenty-one years his wife's senior, he expected a great deal of support from Aurelia Plath in pursuing his research interests in biology and entomology; the first eighteen months of their marriage had been devoted to work on his book *Bumblebees and their Ways* (1934). He stubbornly refused to see a doctor about his medical problems; when he finally yielded, it was discovered that he had *diabetes mellitus*, which might have been cured if detected in time. In 1940 his leg was amputated and he died six weeks later, without leaving hospital. Mrs Plath's reaction was one of determined stoicism: for the children's sake, a mother must not be seen to cry. Her daughter, who had adored her rather awe-inspiring father, interpreted it as lack of caring.

> And this is how it stiffens, my vision of that seaside childhood. My father died, we moved inland. Whereon those nine first years of my life sealed themselves off like a ship in a bottle – beautiful, inaccessible, obsolete; a fine white flying myth. (*Johnny Panic*, p. 124)

The drama of that conclusion modulated into mundane struggle on Mrs Plath's part to keep the family afloat through financial and health difficulties. Sylvia was an A student throughout school; she painted and drew and wrote poems, sharing much of her reading with her mother, who describes their relationship as 'osmotic'. Scholastic achievement counted for a great deal in the family: no doubt the *émigré* inheritance – Otto Plath had come from Grabow, a Prussian town in the Polish corridor, and Aurelia was second-generation Austrian – played its part in this wish to be seen to excel, which Plath never lost. Such need for constant attention and praise is a kind of strait-jacket, especially for an artist.

Accounts of her school and college days emphasize the deliberate, at times driven manner in which she conducted her life. The conventionality and lack of spontaneity are striking. The situation in which Sylvia Plath found herself – a small town in America in the late 1940s and early 1950s – had its cultural as well as personal constraints. She felt she had to balance braininess with beauty, poetry with popularity. The pressures towards conformity and achievement were intensified when she went to Smith College, a single-sex institution with an excellent reputation to which she won a scholarship. By unremitting labours she made her mark,

Mademoiselle college editors, 1953. Plath is the figure at the top of the star, and wrote the caption: '... Issues illuminated: academic freedom; the sorority controversy; our much labeled (and libeled) generation. From our favorite fields, stars of the first magnitude shed a bright influence on our plans for jobs and futures. Although horoscopes for our ultimate orbits aren't yet in, we Guest Eds are counting on a favorable forecast with this send-off from MLLE, the star of the campus.' (Photograph: Landshoff.)

and by her second year was enjoying academic and social success, though the work often made her anxious. In one of the more bubbly letters to her mother, Plath relates her election to an honours society, an invitation to join the editorial board of the *Smith Review*, and the news that W.H. Auden would be at Smith the next year.

> Honestly, Mum, I could just cry with happiness. I love this place so, and there is so much to do creatively, without having to be a 'club woman'. Fie upon offices! The world is splitting open at my feet like a ripe, juicy watermelon. (*Letters Home*, p. 85)

The letters to her mother also describe periods of profound depression, and there is talk of suicide. The main source of information about Plath's breakdown and actual suicide attempt in 1953 is *The Bell Jar*, an unmistakably autobiographical novel (first published under the protecting pseudonym, Victoria Lucas, in 1963). The opening paragraph of the novel refers to the execution by electric chair of the Rosenbergs, American Communists who had been convicted of spying for the Soviet Union. The narrator, Esther Greenwood, says, 'I couldn't help wondering what it would be like, being burned alive all along your nerves'. The novel is an account of just this process, in emotional terms, and includes an impression of the electro-convulsive therapy treatment which Plath underwent. She had gone home for the summer in the hope of attending a writing class at Harvard, but had not been accepted for it. Exhausted by her spell in New York as one of the college guest-editors of *Mademoiselle*, with nothing to fall back on over the long weeks of the vacation, her promise as a writer apparently unrecognized, living with her mother's expectations of self-discipline and work – everything combined to drain away a sustaining self-confidence. Prizes of any kind set up their own momentum, and when that failed, she plummeted down.

Plath took an overdose of sleeping-pills, left a note to say she had gone for a long walk, and crawled under the house. It was not until two days later that her brother located her, alive. Mrs Olive Higgins Prouty, who had endowed Plath's scholarship at Smith, stepped in to pay for her treatment at a Boston psychiatric hospital, McLean. In a sense, as with the 'flying myth' of her childhood, this experience was to be sealed away. Plath had not found a way of integrating the losses, anger and disgust she had explored with Ruth Beuscher, her trusted psychiatrist, into her continuing life.

In 1955 she graduated from Smith *summa cum laude*, with a

Fulbright scholarship to spend two years at Newnham College, Cambridge. Mrs Plath describes these years as 'the most exciting and colourful of Sylvia's life'. Her experience of being an American in England has been regarded with little sympathy by the majority of those writing about her. The shared language tends to disguise the dauntingly foreign quality of that experience: Plath's voracious intelligence did not always grasp the social and intellectual nuances of a very different culture. Academically she did well at Cambridge, working for her BA, and made the most of the dramatic and literary opportunities the university offered. When she encountered Ted Hughes at a Cambridge party in February 1956, Plath clearly felt that she had at last met her equal. Her journal entries and letters to her mother strike a sustained, Lawrentian note of ecstasy. When Mrs Plath came to England in June, she found herself a witness at her daughter's marriage.

Hughes took a teaching job in a Cambridge school, while Plath characteristically juggled her revision for examinations, housekeeping, writing and sending out Hughes's poems to American journals. Her professional approach to his writing, as well as her belief in his 'genius', gave his poetic career an impetus it would otherwise have lacked; she was impatient with English literary cliques and the 'stuffiness' of much contemporary writing, and thought the Americans would be more open and encouraging. This proved to be the case when in 1957 Hughes's *Hawk in the Rain* won a contest run by Harpers Publishing Co. for a best first collection. His confidence in her gifts, his wide range of reading – he went to Cambridge to read English but changed to archaeology and anthropology – and his writerly disciplines were also a great support to her, if dangerously complete: 'always stimulating me to study, think, draw and write. He is better than any teacher, even fills somehow that huge, sad hole I felt in having no father' (*Letters Home*, p. 289).

After Plath finished her degree, they sailed to America where she was to take up a two-year teaching post at Smith. Finding that teaching consumed all her energies, she made the difficult decision to give it up in order to write. By this time Plath had published both poetry and stories in American magazines, conscientiously tailoring her style to suit the publications she targeted. We will look at her reading and the poets who influenced her in Chapter 2, but it would be useful if you now read her poem 'Point Shirley' (p. 110) to get an idea of the kind of poem Plath was writing in 1959, when she was living in Boston.

This is the seascape of her childhood – but how personal is the tone of the poem? What is Plath saying about the 'end of the land', the sea-surge and its connection with her grandmother?

> She is dead
> Whose laundry snapped and froze here, who
> Kept house against
> What the sluttish, rutted sea could do.

The poem shows considerable technical accomplishment: the advance and retreat of the waves and the gravel's resistance is embodied in the alternation of long and short lines; the sibilance of the water conveyed in the frequent 's' alliteration. The end-rhymes are marked, and the emphatic, insistent energy of the poem is reminiscent of Robert Lowell's poetry of the late 1940s, with its similarly clotted syntax – and its recurrent seascapes.

In Boston Plath sat in on Lowell's poetry seminar. When he later wrote the preface to the American edition of *Ariel*, her posthumous collection of poems, he recalled her presence at those classes:

> She was willowy, long-waisted, sharp-elbowed, nervous, giggly, gracious – a brilliant tense presence embarrassed by restraint. Her humility and willingness to accept what was admired seemed at times to give her an air of maddening docility that hid her unfashionable patience and boldness. She showed us poems that later, more or less unchanged, went into her first book, *The Colossus*. They were somber, formidably expert in stanza structure, and had a flair for alliteration and Massachusetts' low-tide dolor.[4]

That image of the flapping laundry was to surface again, two years later, in 'Blackberrying' (p. 168):

> The only thing to come now is the sea.
> From between two hills a sudden wind funnels at me,
> Slapping its phantom laundry in my face.

It has a vivid accuracy that makes it seem inevitable, something that we have always known, waiting for expression. In the context of 'Blackberrying', there is no possibility of its domestic familiarity being in any way reassuring. Please now read the poem, which was among the first Plath wrote when, back in England, the Hughes family moved from London to an old house in Devon. If you associate blackberrying with preservation, perhaps especially with female activities such as jam-making or cooking pies, and if you see it as an essentially attractive activity, then the poem will bring you up sharp. Plath habitually disconcerts her readers. The speaker seems a recalcitrant figure, collecting the fruit in her solitary way. Is she angry? Resentful? Bloody-minded even? Or is she deeply threatened?

From the beginning there is the hope of the sea, held out as a kind of promise in this enclosed landscape – although 'heaving' does not sound promising, it seems to transfer the poet's own nausea at the sheer proliferation and mocking juiciness of the berries. The fruit endeavour to ingratiate themselves, and she resists: 'I had not asked for such a blood sisterhood' – the implication that the juices resemble the menstrual flow is inescapable.

The flies gorged on berries have attained paradise – hog heaven. But the figure will not be delayed or deterred, pressing on for a sight of the sea. There is disbelief and also a momentary relenting in the harried tone of the poem: 'The hills are too green and sweet to have tasted salt' – I think foreigners ('exile that I am') are struck by the way lush pastureland lies alongside the sea in Britain. And then all the colour, which has had the intensity of stained glass, drains out of the poem; the sea fills it with noise and glare in a brilliant finale:

> A last hook brings me
> To the hills' northern face, and the face is orange rock
> That looks out on nothing, nothing but great space
> Of white and pewter lights, and a din like silversmiths
> Beating and beating at an intractable metal.

Thus the space and freedom denied by the blackberry lane – denied perhaps by the conservative role of women, the 'blood sisterhood' – emerges here as something essentially threatening, formidable. It gives nothing back to the onlooker. Might the silversmith stand for the wordsmith, struggling with her resistant medium?

Notice also 'intractable': there are many such words in Plath's poetry – 'unstable', 'inaccessible', 'irretrievable', 'untouchable', 'incoherence'. Sometimes these abstract concepts are in the plural, as though she were willing them into solidity, but they all speak of negatives, they make stability, access, coherence impossible.

What had changed Plath's poetry between *The Colossus*, published in 1960, and 'Blackberrying', written in late September 1961? Her personal circumstances had certainly altered: her daughter, Frieda Rebecca, was born in London on 1 April 1960; her son, Nicholas Farrar, would be born in Devon on 17 January 1962. Hughes suggests that maternity made a crucial difference:

> the truly miraculous thing about her will remain the fact that in two
> years, while she was almost fully occupied with children and house-

keeping, she underwent a poetic development that has hardly any
equal on record for suddenness and completeness. The birth of her
first child seemed to start the process. All at once she could compose
at top speed, and with her full weight.[5]

Being a good mother was immensely important to Plath, and the
consequent restrictions on her time may have focused her poetic
energies to a productive degree. *The Colossus* had good reviews in
England, and Alfred Knopf decided to publish it in America;
British and American journals published her poems, and some
were broadcast on the BBC; she received a sustantial writing grant
from an American foundation. Such recognition, vital to her sense
of herself, was no doubt especially important given the high
reputation Hughes was establishing. But publication, maternity
and country life are insufficient to explain the change in poetic
tone, as well as technique: there is a powerful 'I' in 'Blackberrying'
which is very different from the shadowy presence in 'Point
Shirley' and many of the poems in *The Colossus*.

   If Plath had learned something from Lowell's early style, she
learned more – and used it more independently – from his collection *Life Studies* (1959), one of the books that gave rise to the
critical label 'confessional poetry'. She described this in an interview as the 'breakthrough volume', an

> intense breakthrough into very serious, very personal, emotional
> experience which I feel has been partly taboo. . . . I think particularly
> the poetess Anne Sexton, who writes about her experiences as a
> mother, as a mother who has had a nervous breakdown, is an
> extremely emotional and feeling young woman and her poems are
> wonderfully craftsman-like . . .[6]

Anne Sexton (*To Bedlam and Part Way Back*, 1960; *All My
Pretty Ones*, 1962) had also attended Lowell's poetry seminar,
and her brief memoir of Plath presents a rather tougher character
than Lowell's sketch, a drinking companion in sessions after
class, when suicide methods could be discussed. Although Sexton
demurred at the casual lumping of her own work with Lowell's,
she supposed 'we might have shown [Plath] something about
daring – daring to tell it true. W.D. Snodgrass showed me in the
first place . . .'.[7]

   Why were these American poets – Lowell, Snodgrass (*Heart's
Needle*, 1959), Plath, Sexton and also John Berryman (*77
Dream Songs*, 1964) – called 'confessional'? M.L. Rosenthal, the
American critic who gave the term wide currency, was referring
to the 'series of personal confidences' that *Life Studies* rep-
resented: Lowell's unsparing portraits of his mother and father,

for example. 'Confessional' is often conflated with 'sensational':
the bitterness of Snodgrass's divorce and the painful restructuring
of his relationship with his daughter; Sexton's mental illness; tales
of adultery, alcoholism, madness. The old taboos about reticence
and privacy had been broken, and the resulting poetry is not
usually as rigorously shaped as Snodgrass's syllabics; it tends to be
conversational, colloquial, confiding. In Berryman's poems the
apparent artlessness is emphasized by the use of ampersands and
scarcely any capital letters. Such poetry has the intimacy of a diary
or letter; indeed, Lowell was to scandalize friends as well as
critics by embedding excerpts from private correspondence in his
later poems.

Plath, who had shared with Lowell the experience of hos-
pitalization in McLean (he wrote about it in 'Waking in the Blue',
in *Life Studies*), now suffered an experience common to this group
of poets: a broken marriage. There had always been tensions in
her relationship with her husband, but they came to an explosive
resolution in 1962. Hughes left his wife for another woman, and
moved to London; Plath battled on in Devon, writing like fury.
The midwife had advised her to make use of the time in the early
morning when she couldn't sleep, and that was when many of the
poems in *Ariel* were written: 'I am up about five, in my study with
coffee, writing like mad – have managed a poem a day before
breakfast. All book poems. Terrific stuff, as if domesticity had
choked me', Plath wrote to her mother in October 1962.

Let us look at one of the poems from this period, 'Fever 103°'
(p. 231). Plath glossed this in her BBC introduction as concerning
two kinds of fire: the kind that merely burns, transmuted or
'suffered' into the kind that purifies. I am reminded of two poems
by T.S. Eliot: section IV of *Little Gidding* (*Four Quartets*); and
the notes to *The Waste Land*, quoting the words of St Augustine –
'to Carthage then I came, where a cauldron of unholy loves sang
all about mine ears' – and the lines from Dante's *Purgatorio* –
' "... be mindful in due time of my pain." Then dived he back into
that fire which refines them.' Eliot uses quotations to pick up the
subjects of lust and redemption with tongs, as it were: only the
mediation of ancient authors enables him to deal with matters just
as close to his heart as they are to the more openly 'confessional'
Plath. Although she does not have this protection of impersonality, Plath uses some of the same modernist methods as Eliot:
disjunction of both tone and sense, rapid variations from formal
to colloquial, trying on different voices.

The tongues that are fire and speech have a long lineage, and
Plath draws on that accumulated power of imagery as well as

adding her own, modern myths. She refers to the death of Isadora Duncan, who revolutionized modern dance with her barefoot performances in floating chiffon, and who was choked to death when her long scarf caught in the wheel of a car. Here the wheel could belong to that 'black car of Lethe' from which the speaker steps 'Pure as a baby' in the later poem 'Getting There' (p. 247). It looks as though nothing pure will be found in 'Fever 103°'. If, in traditional theology, we descend to hell's flames on account of sin, then who has sinned, and how, in the poem? Or is it all just feverish chatter? The delirious obsessions of the fevered mind are mimicked in the way words fall in threes and pairs: 'dull', for example, occurs three times, one for each head of Cerberus (the dog guarding hell's gate). The syntax has the quality of jottings: punctuation falls abruptly, explanatory verbs are missing. Everything that falls between the long dashes after 'I think I may rise——' and '. . . petticoats——' is parenthetical to the thrust of the poem, which relies on the rise/Paradise rhyme for its conclusion.

Direct address is characteristic of confessional poetry, but who is the speaker addressing here? Michael Kirkham has suggested that it is her child,[8] perhaps because 'Your body / Hurts me' would be appropriate to childbirth, or to the enormous claims of a child on the physical strength of a parent; even because the innocence of the child's body is painful to the mother who cannot protect it for ever. Still, this seems to me a misreading, given the emphasis on sexual sins in the poem, and the physicality of the speaker's description of her body, flickering like a flame or flushing like a flower. The extravagant claim seems more appropriate to a lover, someone the speaker is trying to burn free of, reconstituting herself as 'a pure acetylene virgin'. Again the action is like that of 'Getting There', 'stepping from this skin / Of old bandages, boredoms, old faces' (p. 249): '(My selves dissolving, old whore petticoats)' – as though the whole burden of being female has to be sloughed off. Plath implies here an unnerving complicity, a readiness to play the required feminine roles, matching masculine promiscuity: a readiness to be victimized. This is a theme to which we will return in Chapter 6. The self-exposure both encourages biographical speculation – does Plath's broken marriage provide the animus for the poem, its manic quality? – and discredits it as a reductive reading of the poetry.

M.L. Rosenthal suggested that confessional poetry put the speaker 'at the centre of the poem in such a way as to make [her] psychological vulnerability and shame an embodiment of [her] civilization'.[9] Do you think this is a good description of what happens in 'Fever 103°'? Do you find the mention of Hiroshima gratuitous or acceptable in this context?

> In these poems, written in the last months of her life and often rushed out at the rate of two or three a day, Sylvia Plath becomes herself, becomes something imaginary, newly, wildly, and subtly created – hardly a person at all, or a woman, certainly not another 'poetess', but one of those super-real, hypnotic, great classical heroines.[10]

Thus Lowell sanctioned the legend of Sylvia Plath, which quickly sprung from her death on 11 April 1963. The painful details of these last months are well known. With winter coming, Plath felt she could not cope in the country, and found a flat to rent in London. It had a blue plaque outside, recording that Yeats had lived there – what better omen? When she moved with the children to 23 Fitzroy Road, she was in high spirits at beginning a new life. Its demands on all her resources, however, were dispiritingly immense. Moreover, the poems she was sending out were slow to be accepted for publication. January 1963 was even colder than January 1939, when Yeats 'disappeared in the dead of winter: / The brooks were frozen . . .'. When Plath saw her doctor late in the month, she admitted to being severely depressed, and on hearing of her earlier history he prescribed a course of anti-depressant drugs. He also arranged for a nurse to help her: when she arrived, she had to break into the flat. Sylvia Plath had gassed herself, her head in the kitchen oven, her children safely in the room above.

The critic A. Alvarez wrote in the *Observer*, 'the loss to literature is inestimable'. She had the manuscript of *Ariel* ready, but it was not published until 1965, edited by Ted Hughes.[11] Alvarez declared: 'The achievement of her final style is to make poetry and death inseparable. . . . Poetry of this order is a murderous art.'[12] This romantic view of her suicide as the stamp of authenticity on her poetry, a view not confined to Alvarez, makes Plath both peculiarly vulnerable and unassailable.

Plath was only thirty-one when she died; the scope of her achievement was controversial then, and nearly thirty years after her death it remains so. To some extent critics are divided along lines of gender – what looks like hysteria to some looks like emotional liberation to others – and of culture – the confessionalism which many British readers find excessive is accepted more easily, even eagerly, by Americans. Her death coincided with the onset of the women's movement, and her life – as much as her art – provided a powerful text for it. Plath's poetry continues to challenge many of our assumptions about how women write (is there such a thing as *l'écriture feminine*?), about the relation of psychological disturbance to art, about the construction of autobiography and the pursuit of authenticity. In the chapters that follow, we will be considering these matters as they arise out of discussions of individual poems, examples of Plath's increasingly daring, discomfiting and compelling work.

2. 'What ceremony of words can patch the havoc?'

Let us begin by looking at some poems of what could be called Plath's apprenticeship. They have an intrinsic interest, but they also show that the power of her best-known poems (written when she was still young) did not emerge with magical suddenness. In high school she read the glossy magazines of the day, *Seventeen* and *Mademoiselle*: unlike her classmates, she was reading them with an eye to publication, studying the form. It took forty-five rejection slips before the first acceptance arrived, from *Seventeen*, in 1950. When she visited a congenial professional writer in the summer of 1952, the message Plath took away was discipline: 1,500 words a day, come what may. Plath's poems of the mid- to late 1950s can be seen as a series of garments tried on and then cast off. Most poets do this – perhaps you have come across Philip Larkin's first collection, *The North Ship*, cut from Yeats's cloth.

The title of this chapter is taken from an early poem, 'Conversation Among the Ruins' (p. 21), and is a question relevant to all of Plath's work: can poetic language contain or control the chaos of experience? Is there a way of bringing order to disordered emotions? She undertakes a cautious investigation in another poem written in 1956, before any of those that went into her first collection, *The Colossus*: 'Miss Drake Proceeds to Supper' (p. 41).

How would you characterize the tone of this poem? Does Plath identify with the woman's predicament when she uses the word 'malice'? Some of the adjective–noun combinations are unexpected (why are the petals unnaturally 'furred'?) – what effect does this have on our perception of objects? Miss Drake has a 'bird-quick eye', but to what purpose? Has she, in the end, become her namesake in her own mind?

DISCUSSION

The tone seems to me both perfectly level and yet inward with the subject. Plath understands – can imagine – the way in which the physical world is full of a menace invisible to the 'normal' eye. The bumps on a table which might cause a glass or plate to slop and spill over, a chair askew that might snag clothes – these are not simply things to watch out for, or put right: they are 'malicious', they intend harm. The menace of everyday objects is something to which Plath continually returns. And what we see as a peculiar gait, shuffling or weaving, is interpreted as part of a ritual to ward off lurking danger, just as a 'normal' person might count paving stones or avoid cracks. Our own perception is slightly skewed by oddities such as the 'unbreakable hummingbirds': the idea seems to belong more appropriately to the eggshells on the previous line. Does its displacement serve to underline that the shells *are* breakable, the birds – reassuringly – not?

The lines between the natural world of roses and birds, wood and sunny air, and the ingrown world of the patient may still be perfectly clear to us, as readers, but we see how they can be blurred. There is empathy of a particular kind at work here, destroying some of our easy assumptions.

Plath has not chosen a complicated verse form or vocabulary here: do any words especially strike you? 'Footing' may seem somewhat archaic. If you look at other poems of this period – 'The Lady and the Earthenware Head' (p. 69), for example – you will see the way her diction sometimes wavers between the contemporary and the Jacobean. It may have been the result of her immersion in the post-Elizabethan dramatists for her Cambridge exams. 'Jag and tooth' set me wondering: T.S. Eliot uses 'jagged' and 'toothed' in a stanza of *Ash-Wednesday* (III, lines 10–11), but this may be mere coincidence. The alliteration is notable, and that remains a strong trait.[1]

Do you detect a flash of humour in the last lines of 'Miss Drake'? Plath certainly expresses a wild kind of humour in her later work, where it is not expected and makes us feel uncomfortable about our reactions. 'Miss Drake Proceeds to Supper', however, is not intended to discomfit in that way: it has good manners. It is quite self-contained, thought-provoking without stepping over any boundaries. After all, what kind of ward is this? A geriatric ward in hospital? A general psychiatric ward? If the latter, might this have been an intimately observed behavioural pattern, observed when Plath herself was in such a ward? Did the empathy arise less from imagination than from a shared, neurasthenic vision? Such questions are simply not raised by the poem, nor answerable from it. Plath's voice is that of an observer: it is not raised, it does not vary, it does not make us wince with its immediacy.

Although she does not use rhyme in this poem, much of her youthful writing does, or is constructed in complicated syllabic patterns; she tried out traditional forms such as the sonnet and the villanelle. All this control of tone and form – what I have called 'good manners' – was the fashion among American 'formalists' of the 1950s. The kind of poetry in which Plath was interested, the kind that won prizes and was published in the polished columns of the *New Yorker* or the *Atlantic Monthly*, belonged in this formalist mode. The Pulitzer Prize in 1956 went to Richard Wilbur, for *Things of This World*: if you are curious about successful American poetry of the period, you might like to look up his work, which Plath admired immensely in the early 1950s.[2]

Formalism was impersonal, balanced, disciplined, graceful: it was the product of a generation that had absorbed the lessons of T.S. Eliot and the New Criticism; in Britain, it had its counterpart in poets of 'The Movement'. Formalist poets were technically accomplished; the strict versification of poets such as Allen Tate and John Crowe Ransom offered them models for their engagement with the difficulty of form.

Plath's 'Conversation Among the Ruins' is a good example of a formalist poem. It uses the structure of the Italian sonnet: it divides into octave (the first eight lines) and sestet (six lines), the break between observation and conclusion signalled by the line space. It follows the traditional rhyme scheme – ABBA ABBA CDE CDE – sometimes using full rhyme, sometimes half-rhyme. The relationship pictured here, according to Hughes's note, is that depicted in a painting by the Italian surrealist Giorgio de Chirico. Do we need to know that? Could it simply be a theatrical rendering of a real parting? What about the image of the man in modern dress contrasted with the woman in classical pose – might that not be a metaphor for the one partner who wishes to cling to a beautifully composed past, and the other who is poised for a different future?

By the end of the decade, Plath had become more critical of such writing, noting that Wilbur's poetry offered 'a fresh speaking and picturing with incalculable grace and all sweet, pure, clear, fabulous, the maestro with the imperceptible marcel. Robert Lowell after this is like good strong shocking brandy after... dessert wine' (*Journals*, p. 292).[3]

The decade could be viewed through quite a different poetic lens: poets such as Charles Olson, Gregory Corso and Lawrence Ferlinghetti were also producing their first books; Allen Ginsberg's *Howl* came out in 1956. These poets were not concerned with disciplining emotion, they took their cue from the uninhibited Walt Whitman, even William Blake, building their verse not on the formal patterns of metre and rhyme but on the basis of breathing – not so free that it lacked a pattern altogether, yet free enough to alter as the thought demanded, as the emotion deepened or lightened, from line to line. Such flexibility could dissolve into prose in the hands of careless poets. Those who used it well produced a speaking voice, sometimes a raging voice, much more intimate with the reader than the formalist poets, who kept a deliberate distance.

We find a kind of intimacy and a deeply unsettling quality in two of Plath's poems from 1957, 'All the Dead Dears' (p. 70) and 'The Disquieting Muses' (p. 74). **Do these poems have anything in common? Are the 'Dead Dears' and the 'Muses' somehow related? What formal changes do you notice, compared with the previous year's two poems? Whose voice repeats 'Mother, Mother' in 'The Disquieting Muses': does it belong to a chiding adult, or an insistent child?**

DISCUSSION

Plath is writing in a long tradition by invoking the Muses: the ancient belief was that there were nine of them, sister-goddesses, who inspired scholars and artists, especially musicians and poets. They were usually portrayed as beautiful young virgins: Plath preferred to associate them with witches and the mad. Male poets often call upon 'the Muse', connecting her inspiration and their current beloved. Feminist critics have pointed out that we are more accustomed to woman as Muse, blowing hot or cold, than to woman as poet, and indeed in this poem the Muses seem hostile to creative effort. Plath conflates them with the fairies that attended the christening of Sleeping Beauty: you remember that seven beautiful fairies were invited but the ugly one was forgotten – and arrived anyway, with her prophecy of destruction. The fairytale world in this poem is the comforting creation of her mother, with its heroic bear, gingerbread witches, even a stiffening of Norse myth: 'Thor is angry: we don't care!' It is a protective, benign world of achievement, except that the speaker falls short – 'could/Not lift a foot in the twinkle-dress', 'my touch oddly wooden in spite of scales'. There is a tug of war going on between what is expected and what has happened: what was inadmissible at the beginning, not pretty enough for the mother's world, has yet smashed its way in and will never leave. Mother floats off, into Never Never Land; the daughter is left with her permanent companions, whose presence she will never reveal. She is trapped by her daughterly training; she is not the only woman who has been brought up not to speak of what is not 'nice'.

It is not simply the title of 'The Disquieting Muses' that makes me describe it as unsettling. Plath remarked in her introduction to a reading of the poem for the BBC that it was taken from a painting by Giorgio de Chirico, whose work particularly appealed to her.

> All through the poem I have in mind the enigmatic figures in this painting – three terrible faceless dressmaker's dummies in classical gowns ... [they] suggest a twentieth-century version of other sinister trios of women – the Three Fates, the witches in *Macbeth*, de Quincey's sisters of madness. (*Collected Poems*, p. 276)

The surrealists were determined to unsettle their audience: they perceived people's mental state as naturally tending towards disorder, and explored the furthest reaches of such states. They used familiar objects in unfamiliar juxtapositions, they combined colours and textures in disorientating ways; objects in their canvases or sculptures seemed a random collection such as we sometimes recall from dreams or nightmares, more real than 'reality'. Does this have any bearing on your reading of the poem?

'All the Dead Dears', too, has a visual inspiration: a stone coffin in the Cambridge Archaeological Museum, with the skeletons of a lady, a mouse and a shrew. What does the title suggest to you? Do the 'dears' and 'darlings' of the poem mean quite the opposite, in fact? Why, then, does Plath use those words?

As in 'The Disquieting Muses', there is a terrible sense of presiding fate, and of the tentacular reach of women, a family embrace that the speaker wants to elude but cannot. History – whether embodied in the family or the larger perspective of the universe – is purely threatening. Men, it would seem, cannot survive in this environment: they drown. One can understand why the absent father and the barnacle mother would be such potent images for Plath.[4] Do they transcend the personal context, in this poem, and exist in their own right?

Poems that mention muses are often about the writing process: there is a sonnet by Sir Philip Sidney about wanting to write a poem to his mistress that would make her take pity on him, 'Loving in truth and fain in verse my love to show'. In his effort to impress her he raids other writers, trying to come up with brilliant and witty images, but to no avail.

> Thus, great with child to speak, and helpless in my throes,
>   Biting my truant pen, beating myself for spite;
>   Fool, said my Muse to me, look in thy heart and write!

It is a well-crafted poem about honesty, and neatly turned – the Muse's instruction is the last line, the poem is written. Plath ends 'The Disquieting Muses' by saying she will keep her muses a secret, but the poem is actually a description of them and the way they set her awry in the world. Could she be saying, too, that the anger she feels, which is such a raw impetus to the later poems, is something her poems will not 'betray'? Does the way this poem is constructed act as a discipline to the feeling released in it? Consider the last stanza, for example, which has the rhythm of a ballad, with ballad-like repetition, 'Mother, mother'. The last line and a half cut off that riding rhythm and clamp down on the whole poem. There is a similar hardness in the alliterative ending of 'All the Dead Dears'.

If there is one myth that Plath destroys, surely it is the myth of the 'inspired' poet, who writes as though receiving dictation from the Muse. She drafted and redrafted her poems. The methods Plath used to set her imagination going were enlarged in her marriage by suggestions and exercises from Hughes. It is as though she were still the brilliant pupil, going through the examination hoops.[5] You may like to look at her early poem 'Sow' (p. 60) together with his 'View of a Pig' to see whether the two poets have anything in common: Plath said that although they criticized each other's work, 'we write poems that are as distinct and different as our fingerprints themselves must be'.[6] One aspect of her work that owed much to Hughes's prompting was an interest in the spirit world and psychic phenomena, ways of tapping the unconscious that bypass the controls of consciousness. He gave her tarot cards, they used a Ouija board (there is a comically practical note about this by Hughes in the *Collected Poems*), she read books about folklore that opened on to a world of archetypal images. It may be that he thought this was a way out of her personal world, a route to the supra-personal, but with Plath it did not work in that way: archetypes tended to be confirmations rather than transformations of the way she saw her personal history.

Dreams had always fascinated her. When she decided to stop teaching at Smith and move to Boston in order to write, she took a job at Massachusetts General Hospital for two months, typing records in the psychiatric clinic. These were partly dream transcriptions; the kind of material they provided can be seen in 'Johnny Panic and the Bible of Dreams'.

Such preoccupations were nourished, too, by an admiration for Yeats, and for those very aspects of his work that the New Criticism tended to downplay: his use of myth and legend, his sense of the spirit world. As you may know, Yeats encouraged his wife, when they were newly married, in automatic writing.

In December 1958 Plath had decided to resume sessions with Dr Ruth Beuscher, the psychiatrist who had won her trust at the time of her suicide attempt. Her extremely controlled social self, her masks, could be set aside in these explorations of her relationship with her father and mother, especially her mother – 'So I feel terrific. In a smarmy matriarchy of togetherness it is hard to get sanction to hate one's mother, especially a sanction one believes in' (*Journals*, p. 266) – of her fear of writing, of her stubborn wish for recognized academic achievement, of 'how to express anger creatively'. The therapy ended in the spring, when Plath and Hughes set off to drive across America; they then went to stay for eleven weeks at Yaddo, the artists' colony in upstate New York. The poems she wrote there, most critics think, are a sign that she had found her true direction.

Please read 'The Manor Garden' (p. 125) and 'Mushrooms' (p. 139). **What does Plath mean in her lines about history in the first poem? Is there an imperfect development there, something that fails to emerge from the shadows? Does the list of things inherited rely on a knowledge of the poet's personal history if it is to appear other than random, even meaningless?**

DISCUSSION

'The Manor Garden' mingles birth and death in the long perspective of evolution: without Hughes's note, would you have guessed immediately that this was a poem about human gestation? 'Your day approaches' being juxtaposed with 'Incense of death' throws us off the right scent, perhaps. 'The pears fatten like little buddhas': so too does the mother, but the wonderfully ripe image of passivity is not developed, simply left to hang on the branch.

The foetus develops, a microcosm, gradually taking its human shape. This approaching birth seems far from the fresh start, the clean slate that Plath will later celebrate. Stars 'Already yellow the heavens'; like yellowing paper this suggests ageing rather than warmth (perhaps Plath was thinking of Van Gogh's 'Starry Night', though, where the yellow pools of stars are energetic); everything is coming to an end, and the omens of spider and worm are not friendly. What is the crow's place?

It may be that we expect protectiveness in a poem concerned with pregnancy, and are disconcerted by the air of detachment – there is nothing explicit to link the foetus with the poet / mother – and the brooding landscape.

'Mushrooms', Plath noted in her journal, was an exercise she set herself, but had no sense of it as a success or failure until Hughes said he liked it. **What do you make of it? What is the force of the biblical quotation at the end of the poem? Is there a hint of gaiety, or only of menace?**

DISCUSSION

Plath probably saw mushrooms sprouting in the damp autumn days she spent at Yaddo, but the poem seems particularly apt to those ubiquitous, featureless mushrooms on sale in supermarkets. See how the lines of the poem themselves, apparently timid – short, unemphatic – multiply and multiply. They may be meek, but they are relentless. They may be as bland as tables or shelves, yet they are confident they will inherit the earth. If we are used to thinking of the Beatitudes as comforting – 'Blessed are the meek; for they shall inherit the earth' (Matthew 5:3) – then this poem provides quite a different perspective. Mushrooms grow in dark, moist places; they push their way through. Plath touches on their sexual symbolism in stanzas five and six: the phallic mushroom shape takes on the characteristics of the sexually aggressive male. Is it too far-fetched to link this menacing behaviour with the mushroom cloud? Plath was certainly very conscious of the nuclear issue, and often presented it in terms of a male conspiracy.

When she was interviewed for a Library of Congress recording in April 1958, and asked what poetry she read, Plath answered: 'Yeats, Ted Hughes continually, Yeats, Eliot, John Crowe Ransom. I have started reading Robert Lowell.... Who else, Ted? Yes, Hopkins.' Asked what she valued in Yeats, she replied:

> I first learnt changing in sound, assonance, from Yeats...I read Dylan Thomas a great deal for subtlety in sound. I never worked at anything but rhyme before, very rigid rhymes, and I began to develop schemes and patterns for sounds which were somehow less obvious.[7]

The sound variations in Hopkins's and Thomas's poetry do not occur in isolation from both men's intense perceptions of the natural world. Hopkins's homage to the specific was a part of his religious vision of particularities created by God: care over sound was a way of giving each word its distinct place in the poem as each object had in creation. Even when delight failed him, his despair was brilliantly articulated. Thomas's extravagant pleasure in natural phenomena was matched by his verbal powers; his own vision of paradise was intimately related to childhood, a time out of time, a time before the individual suffers separation from nature. Do you think that the two poets' vision of the natural world has anything in common with Plath's? You may want to glance back at the poems mentioned in Chapter 1.

At Yaddo, Plath also attentively read the poetry of Theodore Roethke (1908–63), and his influence on her poems is marked. Like Thomas, Roethke had a vision of oneness with nature and, like Hopkins, an eye for its minutest detail. But his vocabulary was less gorgeous, and his sense of his readers was much more acute: he talked directly to them, he exclaimed, he gloomed, he did not mind appearing foolish. Eric Homberger characterizes Roethke as wanting 'access to the deepest recesses of personality, sensibility and psychic energy – and even beyond that to the primal roots of growth, nurture and biological existence'.[8] Obviously at this time, having recently undergone psychoanalysis, and knowing that she was pregnant, such subjects were peculiarly fascinating to Plath as poetic material. Besides that, Roethke's poems offered a subtly shifting metrical stress that extended the lessons of Yeats. Plath's journal entry for 22 October 1959 records:

> Ambitious seeds of a long poem made up of separate sections: Poem on birthday. To be a dwelling on madhouse, nature: meanings of

> tools, greenhouses, florists shops, tunnels, vivid and disjointed.
> An adventure. Never over. Developing. Rebirth. Despair. Old
> women. Block it out. (*Journals*, p. 322)

And the next day:

> an exercise begun, in grimness, turning into a fine, new thing: first of
> a series of madhouse poems. October in the toolshed. Roethke's
> influence, yet mine (*Journals*, p. 323).

Please read 'Poem for a Birthday' (p. 131), bearing Plath's comment in mind. **Does it describe the poem she eventually wrote?
What is the role of fertility in the poem? What is the relation between the world of humans and the world of plants and animals?
What is it about the way 'Poem for a Birthday' is written that
makes it so disturbing? Is it the abruptness, often a line a sentence,
and all the end-stopping which prevents a flow, emphasizes
disconnection?**

DISCUSSION

The motive tension of 'Poem for a Birthday' is something Roethke
could not experience: a desire to remain in a womb-like space, in
the dark, and the knowledge that Plath herself is a womb, willy-
nilly impelling a child towards light; a defiant, sometimes frantic
rejection of the mother, and the unstoppable journey towards
motherhood. Something that has broken has to be mended, and
identifying the self with natural processes, or with flowers and
roots – as Roethke can, in a healing way – will not work for this
poet, beset by questions of identity. 'Who' sets the tone of the
poem. What tugs at her from the underground is the underworld
of the mad – with its inmates who *do* hibernate, halls 'full of
women who think they are birds' (remember 'Miss Drake'), where
'they light me up like an electric bulb'. The speaker has lost
control over herself, she is in the hands of others who choose what
to do with her. This sense of being a mere object is a recurrent
torment to Plath.

A sequence allows a poet to approach the same core of
experience from different angles, it can be less of a linear pro-
gression, more of a circling; a way of going deeper and then
abandoning the attempt for a new one. It often makes the reader
work harder. Try taking a recurrent image and following it
through the poems: the mouth, for example. In psychoanalytical
terms, the oral stage is pre-Oedipal, before the child begins to
assume a separate identity from the mother, and when much of its
sense of the world is mediated through the mouth. 'I am all

mouth', in the second line: voracious, that says, and dependent, but perhaps behind the phrase there is a vernacular expression lurking, 'You've got a big mouth', you talk too much. So the speaker takes in and gives out an enormous amount: too much to cope with.

> Mother you are the one mouth
> I would be tongue to. Mother of otherness
> Eat me. Wastebasket gaper, shadow of doorways.

Here the mouth opens in order to swallow: the real mouth, the wastepaper basket that takes all the rejects, the doorway into which people step and may be gone forever. A desired retreat to the womb, to childhood ('being small'), combines with a terror of being absorbed into the mother: that verb 'would' is perfectly ambiguous – it can be read as 'would like to', it can be read accusingly, 'to you, I would simply' be a tongue, thus as giving expression to the mother's life, not her own.

In 'Dark House', the vegetable world reaches down a layer to where, insanely (?) insouciant, 'Moley-handed, I eat my way'. Abruptly – 'All-mouth licks up the bushes / And the pots of meat' – the speaker dissociates herself from this devouring thing, who yet seems harmless enough, 'a fat sort'. But 'Maenad', the third section, jumps out of the greenhouse and into the fire. Maenads in classical legend were the female followers of Dionysus, and worked themselves into a frenzy during which they might dis-member any onlookers. Those could be the others, their limbs askew, in the last stanza. Plath may have in mind, too, the episode in which the Maenads tore apart Orpheus, poet and musician; as his head floats down river, it keeps singing. The mouth persists in making its sounds. 'The mother of mouths didn't love me' – petulance or flat statement? Plath's tone is often difficult to pin down. The speaker wants to consume, but the 'berries of the dark' she desires are the opposite of what she will be made to swallow, time's 'endless glitter'.

What place does 'The Beast' have, then, in this cycle? What do all the formulaic names mean? How does this section work? Is it more of an incantation, a reduction, or a way of providing the speaker in the end with the name she pleaded for in the previous poem?

In 'Flute Notes from a Reedy Pond', 'frog-mouth and fish-mouth drink / The liquor of indolence': the insistent beat of the poem slows to a slither of s's, as though the pond-water has at last provided a rest-station, 'something safer' than death. But it is only temporary: water and fire alternate. The 'Witch Burning' has a domestic image of food – rice grains in a pot of boiling water – turned to an extraordinary purpose. The speaker herself, swelling with pregnancy, is forbidden to be inert as the heat is turned up and the lick of the flame renders the pain of giving birth. The 'mouth of a door', the 'mouth of a flame': devouring dark or devouring light, inescapable one way or another.

The note of exaltation at the end of 'Witch Burning' is entirely absent from the opening of 'The Stones': the speaker has fallen out of 'the robes of all this light' into 'the stomach of indifference', where she lies like a stone. The image has the force of personal experience behind it – Plath herself crawled under the house, you remember, in her suicide attempt, and the mouth-hole involuntarily gave her away. The city of menders, however, is cheerfully indifferent in another sense, indifferent to her stony desire to be left alone: 'The food tubes embrace me.' The Muses in her earlier poem had 'heads like darning eggs' (again the domestic item turned to sinister ends); here, too, the nurse is bald, but 'love is [her] uniform'. Does 'The Stones' seem a somehow logical culmination of the sequence, or simply another element in a collage of experience, no more or no less final than the others?

Unlike Roethke, whose poems are instinct with celebration, Plath looks to nature for dissolution and is thwarted. 'Wingy myths' – I take this to mean myths of resurrection or at the least of flying, that is, of hope and creativity – return here in a second-hand form: people can be put back together again, but not by natural processes. They come to the 'city of spare parts', a place like those surreal canvases where heads and gloves and anatomical bits and pieces are scattered about. Elsewhere Plath uses the image of a flower for the heart – as earlier, the 'stopped geranium': here it is a rose in a cracked vase, and the vase is the speaker. Neither devourer nor devoured, she is the container. Is the last line defiant, determined, resigned – or merely a parroting of what she has been told?

This sequence comes at the end of Plath's first published volume, *The Colossus*. Hughes has described her working method:

> In her earlier poems, Sylvia Plath composed very slowly, consulting her Thesaurus and Dictionary for almost every word, putting a slow, strong ring of ink around each word that attracted her. Her obsession with intricate rhyming and metrical schemes was part of the same process. Some of those early inventions of hers were almost perverse, with their bristling hurdles.[9]

The more you read of the first third of the *Collected Poems*, the more sense this description makes. 'Poem for a Birthday' seems to arise from a different matrix, as though the controlling hand and certainly the dictionary search had been pushed aside. What began as an exercise, freeing the unconscious and its apparently arbitrary associations, became a harrowing exploration of a world of emotions and experiences increasingly difficult to handle.

If you are outwardly set on a successful course – a published, prize-winning author, with a string of academic achievements, married to a prize-winning author, about to have a child – and if that success is not measured simply by imposed criteria but by powerfully internalized standards; if you are also deeply distrustful of all these signs of established identity, which may be removed at any time, and have been through an experience of self-destruction that cannot be obliterated by any mending process (and perhaps still beckons), then your poetry strains and cracks against the language and civilities of formalism.

'The Stones', Hughes said, was a glimpse of a poetic world to which Plath tried to find her way back. Should we characterize this world, and Plath's poetic strategies, as particularly feminine? Acknowledgement of what is hidden, of what is confusing, imitating in the writing itself a sense of confusion; deliberately blurring boundaries between consciousness and the unconcious; an interest in fluid, intermediary states; the representation of many voices rather than a single, knowing voice – all these things, feminist critics would say, are typical of women's writing. Plath had already shown herself perfectly capable of more conventional structure, but it was not appropriate to what she needed to convey in these poems of nature and the madhouse. They are intentionally jarring. The way the individual poems stop and start, abruptly shift, do not follow logical rules of construction – all these things, we can also say, are the typical marks of a Modernist poem. They allow the unconscious to break through the rational defences of conventional meaning: the 'mutinous weather', as Plath put it in her early poem 'Spinster' (p. 49), has broken through 'the barricade of barb and check' conscientiously erected by the apprentice. When her own voices emerge, they speak of unexpected, unwanted, unlovely things.

3. Poet and Mother

In this chapter I want to focus on a group of poems about children and motherhood: 'Metaphors' (p. 116), 'You're' (p. 141), 'Morning Song' (p. 156), 'Mary's Song' (p. 257) and 'Nick and the Candlestick' (p. 240). Does such a focus strike you as a sexual stereotype? Please read the poems now, and think about the attitudes to motherhood they evoke, the images of children they offer, and the variety of verse techniques they employ.

Plath certainly thought that having a child was essential to womanhood, and this was not merely the pressure of social expectation, although that was strong. Adrienne Rich, whose first collection of poems was published in the prestigious Yale Series of Younger Poets in 1951, and of whose work Plath was competitively aware, has written perceptively about the apparently incompatible states of being a woman and a writer in their generation:

> Because I was determined to prove that as a woman poet I could also have what was then defined as a 'full' woman's life, I plunged in my early twenties into marriage and had three children before I was thirty. There was nothing overt in the environment to warn me: these were the fifties, and in reaction to the earlier wave of feminism, middle-class women were making careers of domestic perfection... the family was in its glory.[1]

Plath's letters and journals show that she expected to achieve just such 'domestic perfection'; moreover, she felt that biological and literary creativity were intimately related. In 1957 she declared, 'I will write until I begin to speak my deep self, and then have children, and speak still deeper. The life of the creative mind first, and then the creative body' (*Journals*, p. 166). What may be a handy metaphor for men – Philip Sidney is one of many who have written about themselves as pregnant with poetry – is an overwhelmingly physical experience for women. The connection between giving birth and producing poems is nowhere clearer than in 'Stillborn' (p. 142):

O I cannot understand what happened to them!
They are proper in shape and number and every part.
They sit so nicely in the pickling fluid!
They smile and smile and smile and smile at me.
And still the lungs won't fill and the heart won't start.

Unusually for Plath, the metaphor is absolutely plain and does not alter: do you think it is too contrived? When you read 'Stillborn', you will notice that the third stanza returns to the fish/pig evolution we saw in 'The Manor Garden'. She may well have in mind the pre-'Stones' poems: they 'sit so nicely', are polite, give no indication of distress. Plath quite often uses an exclamatory construction: what effect do you think it has?

Without being sentimental, Plath customarily presents babies as blessings (with the notable, harrassed exception of the late poem 'Lesbos'), and sterility as a curse. Sandra Gilbert suggests that while one might think of a child as confining the mother/poet to her stereotypical role,

In fact, for Plath the baby is often a mediating and comparatively healthy image of freedom (which is just another important reason why the Plath Myth has been of such compelling interest to women), and this is because in her view the fertile mother is a queen bee, an analog for the fertile and liberated poet...[2]

As we have seen, 'Poem for a Birthday' is actually deeply ambiguous in its attitude towards daughter turning mother: is the same true of 'Metaphors'? One critic has said that except for the last line, this is 'pure silliness'; another that it is 'absurd and touching ... like some child's drawing of its mother'. What do you think? What effect does the last line have? The same technique – a series of metaphors in apparently random succession – is used to playful and affectionate effect in 'You're' (p. 141), written a couple of months before her daughter's birth. **In looking at those two poems, do not be misled by their playfulness: how are they constructed? What use does she make of rhythm and rhyme?**

DISCUSSION

Playfulness does not exclude artfulness: 'Metaphors', pretending to be a 'riddle' in nine syllables, has nine lines, each with nine syllables. Its exuberance, even absurdity, is gradually curbed: 'I've eaten a bag of green apples' is both a reference to shape and also to sharp stomach pains (and, perhaps, to the apple Eve ate: the end to a life in paradise and the beginning of a heavy responsibility); again there is a disturbing sense of passivity, of no longer

Sylvia Plath and her daughter Frieda, December 1962

being in control of her own life but hurtled forward in a train she had no means to stop.

In 'Metaphors', the pregnant woman is the loaf; in 'You're'; the baby itself is likened to rising bread. The rhythm and rhyme are not immediately obvious in 'You're': Plath makes her readers work, often puzzling them with a dazzling surface.

> Snug as a bud and at home
> Like a sprat in a pickle jug.
> A creel of eels, all ripples.

The rhymes do not fall where you expect them, but they bind the lines, and there is an absent rhyme as well: 'snug as a bug (in a rug)', we say, only to have that expectation thwarted by 'bud'. Incidentally, notice how the pickling process turns benign in this poem: in 'Stillborn' it embalms failures, here it preserves liveliness. The assonance works to enforce the similes, too: 'Wrapped up in yourself like a spool, / Trawling your dark as owls do'. The long 'o' sounds mimic the owl's hoot.

There are surprisingly few poems about children from their parents' point of view, at least until the second half of this century, but there is a powerful tradition of poets writing about themselves as children. These mainly centre on a sense of what is lost in growing up, from Henry Vaughan in the seventeenth century – 'Happy those early days! when I / Shined in my Angel-infancy' – to Dylan Thomas in the twentieth – 'Now as I was young and easy under the apple boughs / About the lilting house and happy as the grass was green...'. Of course one of the most affecting images in any culture is that of a mother with her baby, but in the West especially it has the force of an icon. The first of these subjects – her own infancy – offers nothing to Plath: when she finds her way back to childhood in the poems it is the womb she heads for, the stage before separation. The second, however, provides the groundnote for several of her poems. The Virgin Mary, as traditionally presented, is the startling exception to Plath's anguished generalization that 'perfection is terrible, it cannot have children'.

In 'Morning Song' the sentiments are secular: a tender poem or a chilly poem, do you think? What images bear out your judgement of the tone? How would you characterize the speaker's relationship to her child? Does it conform to a conventional notion of mother and baby? How does the image of the cloud in the third stanza function within the poem?

DISCUSSION

It has a wonderfully comforting opening, a feeling of reassuring prosperity echoed later in the mention of a 'Victorian nightgown'. The eighteenth-century theory of God as watchmaker, with the universe as his timepiece, is coldly mechanical; here it is love – certainly the parents', but perhaps God's is not ruled out – that makes the new human being tick. Yet that cosy feeling is modulated almost immediately: after all, this process of nature takes its place among the unbiddable elements. And then, in a typically rapid shift, the baby becomes an exhibit, a 'new statue'. What does Plath mean by saying 'your nakedness shadows our safety'?

I should like you to compare two explorations of the idea that a helpless baby is nevertheless a threat to its parents, that it spells an end as well as a beginning, by looking at another poem alongside Plath's, 'My Son, My Executioner' by Donald Hall. Does the form he has chosen – three, regularly rhymed quatrains – indicate a different approach to the subject of parenthood?

> My son, my executioner,
>   I take you in my arms,
> Quiet and small and just astir
>   And whom my body warms.
>
> Sweet death, small son, our instrument
>   Of immortality,
> Your cries and hunger document
>   Our bodily decay.
>
> We twenty-five and twenty-two,
>   Who seemed to live forever,
> Observe enduring life in you
>   And start to die together.[3]

'My Son, My Executioner' is self-consciously cast in the mould of a sixteenth-century poem (cf. Ben Jonson's touching elegy on his first son), meditating on a theme: it could be any father to any son; is Plath's similarly stereotypical? Adrienne Rich, Hall's exact contemporary, has remarked of her own poetry from this period: 'formalism was part of the strategy – like asbestos gloves, it allowed me to handle materials I couldn't pick up bare-handed'.[4] Hall's poem handles a potentially distressing recognition with composed tenderness, but none of the precise physicality of Plath's descriptions of the baby's 'moth-breath', the mouth 'open clean as a cat's', and of herself, 'cow-heavy and floral'. She is prepared to mock her maternal image in a way that is atypical of fathers in poetry, who are more likely to feel their authority and masculinity

solemnly confirmed by the event of a child. Nevertheless, both
Plath and Hall in their different ways open a perspective longer
than their own lives: it may be this idea of succeeding generations
that Plath evokes with her 'drafty museum', in which the parents
'stand round blankly as walls'. It is a surprising reversal of the old
idea that children were blank slates on which time and experience
would make their marks: what does it suggest?

'I'm no more your mother...' – if the experience of
motherhood / parenthood can be viewed as a joyful entry into the
ongoing river of humanity, the baby as a means to immortality, as
Hall maintains, then it can also be seen as an anonymous process,
an indistinguishable part of the natural flow. It makes as little
impression on the larger world as a cloud coming and going. Put
this way, it seems quite a serene image, but it does not function
that way entirely. 'No more' is disturbingly ambiguous: it suggests
'hardly at all', 'no longer'; the connection between parent and
child seems to become ever more tenuous.

Alice Ostriker has argued that the connection of motherhood
with effacement of the self is part of a nexus of female imagery
that dwells on absence and a sense of missing identity: that the
self-sacrificing, nurturing role epitomized in motherhood is the
role which women are expected to play generally in society, thus
the sense of puzzlement and loss found in their poetry.[5] You may
find that the stanza will accommodate both meanings. In the work
of the seventeenth-century metaphysical poets, images were often
'yoked by violence together', and wrenching them into connection is part of the reader's pleasure in the poem, as in Plath's
'Metaphors'. But poets can leave their images as suggestively
ambiguous rather than mutually exclusive terms of a debate.

Plath's metaphors are often grounded in hidden vernacular
perceptions: 'A far sea moves in my ear' – we say that an ear is
'shell pink', and Plath's sentence condenses the simile, connecting
the baby's breathing with the sea. If you recall the mention of the
sea as breath in 'Ocean-1212-W', then it is not too fanciful, I
think, to read the phrase also as a memory of childhood, distant in
time and in space.

She does not linger here, she moves to the particular moment
of early morning feeding. The window anticipates the baby, but
what it feeds off is colour; the baby's first cries are hungry,
demanding, yet gaily interpreted: 'The clear vowels rise like bal-
loons'. The poem lifts off into possibilities at the end.

This conjunction of solitary mother, crying child, the cold hours
of night or morning, seems to have been a poetically fertile one for

Plath. Perhaps exhaustion removed some defences, let the sub-conscious play of association go unchecked. It is a time when boundaries are fluid between sleep and waking, light and shadow, when the maternal instinct of protection is nervously alive to everything that threatens a child's security. Here Plath turns not to myth but to the Christian image of mothering: 'This haloey radiance' is how she describes the candlelight, mirrored, in which she soothes her crying son ('By Candlelight'). There is a more extended comparison worked out in 'Nick and the Candlestick', but before we turn to that poem, let us take a look at 'Mary's Song' (p. 257), written during that burst of creation in the months preceding Plath's death. **How does it differ from 'Morning Song'? What precipitates the shift from the prosaic to the cosmic in the poem? What is the force of the participles in the third stanza? How does Plath use the 'persona' of Mary?**

DISCUSSION

From the Sunday roast to the holocaust: it is a swift trajectory and a kind of parody of Plath's range. The title immediately suggests Christ's mother, and traditionally Mary's song is her response to the angel of the Annunciation, the 'Magnificat', a song of rejoicing in the renewal of the covenant between God and the children of Israel, to be incarnated in Mary's child. (This is usually said or sung in the Anglican church at Evensong, which was the service Plath attended occasionally in Devon.) But of course it also brings to mind the nursery rhyme 'Mary had a little lamb', and there is a gallows humour in that association since Mary's son is the Lamb of God.

He is the sacrificial lamb: in the poem, the lamb itself 'sacrifices its opacity'. Presumably it is that moment of the fat's becoming transparent – as the crackling does – that Plath descri-bes in the next stanza, 'A window, holy gold'; although I also have in mind one of those gas cookers with a window, which catches the light of the flames within. The fire, anyway, turns the lamb from raw meat to cooked, makes of the living lamb a sacrifice in the religious context, and plays over the flesh of those condemned: the heretics judged by the medieval Church; gas, rather than flames, surrounds the Jews delivered up by the Nazis to the extermination ovens. That terrible sense of something gone awry already set in motion by the one word 'cracks' (if the lamb had 'crackled', we would not have been perturbed), expands here under pressure of 'tallow'. Tallow is the material of candles, and the right context for candles is a church; the specifically Catholic context, moreover, is their burning in front of a statue of Mary or another saint, representing a prayer. Here the heretics become human candles – we think barbarously, they thought justly – lit in the name of Mary's son. By using the participles 'melting', 'ousting', Plath suggests that the smoke of these sacrifices never clears: 'They never die'.

Or rather, it is Mary who speaks of the 'gray birds' that settle, reducing everything to ashes. There is nothing redemptive here. Man, whose ingenuity has 'emptied one man into space', has used the same skill to bank the killing ovens. If this is, as I read it, a reference to an astronaut (the first manned space flight had taken place in April 1961, the year before the poem was written) it is surpassingly bleak by virtue of the verb Plath has chosen; its bleakness is compounded by the association of that 'one man' with Christ, headed for the heavens but in the traditional account first descending through space to hell.

> It is a heart,
> This holocaust I walk in,
> O golden child the world will kill and eat.

Whose voice do we hear in this final stanza? The gospel according to St Luke says that Mary 'heard all these things, and pondered them in her heart': in paintings she is often shown in a pensive mood, as though seeing beyond the sombre or playful child on her lap to his heart-breaking death. The emotive connotations of the word 'holocaust' and Plath's appropriation of them is something we'll return to in the next chapter. Here she has apparently avoided these issues by making the song Mary's, and after all the sentiments were and are not peculiar to Plath. In 1960 Plath took Frieda on her first outing, joining a Ban-the-Bomb march in central London:

> I felt proud that the baby's first real adventure should be as a protest against the insanity of world-annihilation. Already a certain percentage of unborn children are doomed by fallout and no one knows the cumulative effects of what is already poisoning the air and sea. (*Letters Home*, p. 378)

So the meaning of holocaust here, even without that personal indication of deep anxiety about nuclear proliferation, is widened from the specific fate of the Jews in the Second World War to the more general potential of universal conflagration. Still, it leaves us with an identity of 'heart' and 'holocaust' that does not quite fit. The speaker seems to be saying that her own emotional life – her heart – is subject to the kind of devastation and punishing sacrifice, to the victimization in fact, suffered by Christ and later

innocents: all their fates are conflated. Can we sustain the belief –
perhaps fragile from the start – that this is indeed in Mary's
persona, or do we hear Plath's own despair breaking through?
This is less a case of Plath's thinking herself into another woman's
mind than of using a particular woman, and all she stands for, as
a point of departure, a ground from which to explore the feelings
of both mother and victim. Her readiness to see herself as victim is
unnerving.

Let us move on to a poem from the same period, addressed to
Plath's son, 'Nick and the Candlestick' (p. 240). The note in
Collected Poems quotes from Plath's introduction to the poem in
a radio broadcast, and signals her intention as to how the poem
should be read. Some critics are very wary of the concept of
'intentionality'. T.S. Eliot, when asked once what he meant by
'Lady, three white leopards sat under a juniper-tree' (*Ash-
Wednesday*, II) replied that he meant 'Lady, three white leopards
sat under a juniper-tree', shutting the door firmly in the critic's
face. Or at least saying that whatever you make of it is up to you,
all I take responsibility for is the words on the page. When Plath
was at university the work of the American New Critics – John
Crowe Ransom, Cleanth Brooks and W.K. Wimsatt in particular
– was becoming the new orthodoxy. Wimsatt published an essay,
'The Intentional Fallacy' (1946), in which he stated that knowledge of the author's intentions was 'neither available nor desirable';[6] even when it seemed to be available, as in the statement by
Plath, it was likely to be misleading. Biography and history were
not relevant: the words on the page were what counted, the text
itself. The difficulty of this position, although it was a healthy
corrective to the purely expressive reading of poetry, is that it
seems to narrow our reading and to suggest that there is one ideal
interpretation awaiting formulation. An expressive approach, on
the other hand, takes the position that the author had an idea, or
an emotion – stage one – and then expressed it in words – stage
two. More recent criticism, much influenced by linguistic theory,
concentrates on the role of language as inseparable from thought:
language does not imitate thought, it is a condition of thinking.
Graham Wallas usefully, if somewhat patronisingly, caught this in
his *Art of Thought* (1926): 'The little girl had the making of a
poet in her who, being told to be sure of her meaning before she
spoke, said: "How can I know what I think till I see what I say?"'
With this insight, we can see poems – and fiction and plays – as
more exploratory works, less fixed in their meanings, indeed
changing their meanings for readers across time and cultures.

Please bear these possible approaches in mind as you read
'Nick and the Candlestick', and 'By Candlelight' (p. 236), written
a few days earlier. Notice that in the former poem she uses the
three-line stanza that is characteristic of her work in 1962. You
might think about the poetic advantages it offers, and the tone
such a construction favours in comparison with the longer stanzas
and individual lines of the preceding year.

DISCUSSION

The first, surprising statement sets the tone for 'Nick and the
Candlestick': a descent into darkness, a search for something
precious. I say surprising because the premiss of the poem is 'I am
a mother', and for the reader all sorts of expectations flow from
that premiss.[7] 'I am a miner' brooks no contradiction: there is no
softening 'I see myself as . . .', or 'Like a miner'. This feeding at
night is a perilous proceeding. It is so cold that the candleflame
hesitates to turn yellow – we are half-way through the poem
before it 'heartens'. Even the candlewax is a product of the dark.
Its sluggish growth is countered by the brisk 'bat air' – the syllables are sharp, like the coldness itself, and then they slowly
descend and lengthen into 'cold homicides'. A deathly tempera-
ture, clinically described. Perhaps the image of the plums in the
next line was suggested by the squashy shape of bats, hanging
from trees like curious fruit.

But what are the newts doing in this white cave – the child's
pale room – and why does Plath associate them with 'holy Joes'?
Is it that in this old house (a biographical fact imported: do we
need to know it?) things still scuttle about in the shadows? It is a
cryptic poem: the rapidity of association may remind you of
'Poem for a Birthday', but the organization is tighter and the
assertion at the end is unequivocal this time. If I unpack some of
the associations here, the riddling quality of the first half of the
poem remains; in the second half, the tone alters.

From 'holy Joes' – parsons, or pious people, an American
expression such as Plath rarely uses – the poem moves to fish: the
ancient symbol of Christianity, scrawled on walls in caves where
persecuted Christians took refuge, and thus to 'Christ!', as though
the speaker has been jerked out of the train of association by
the physical impact, the touch of ice closing in. Look at those
five lines, full of *i*'s; it's a sharp vowel, offering no inducement
to linger. From knives back to fish – the preying piranha – but
the fish changes from noun to adjective over the line break, 'A

piranha / religion', and it feeds off living flesh. The communicant, too, feeds off the flesh of Christ, drinks his blood: wrenched out of its sacred context, the action has a certain barbarity, and more than a touch of the absurd.

But the candle straightens, and out of this dark, rapacious world comes the warm address to the baby, a tone of caress, the unexpected endearment – 'ruby'. And although the religious symbolism retains its darker aspect – the baby's 'crossed position' in the womb picking up the reference to Christ, no sooner conceived than carrying the seed of his death on the Cross – it is also cleansed: the child is a flower, a jewel. It is 'the baby in the barn'.[8]

Roles are reversed. Compare this perspective with that offered by the First Voice in the long dialogue *Three Women* (p. 176); there the mother expresses wonder at the sleeping babies in the hospital ward – 'Can nothingness be so prodigal?' – and anxiety – 'How long can I be a wall around my green property?'. In 'Nick and the Candlestick' it is the mother who is the space, looking to 'the one solid' for confirmation of her identity. The poem is written out of a particular pain, but its focus is pulled clear of that, so that the sense of claustrophobia which sometimes closes off Plath's poems from the reader – especially some of the 1962 poems which seem too private, too indwelling, making us into voyeurs – is absent here. There is a painterly approach, as there is in 'By Candlelight', which reads like a detail of the larger picture in this slightly later poem. Within the controlled form the tonal and associative range is impressively broad, from its authoritative, flat opening to the final wide 'a' vowel repeated, in a security snatched from all the visible and invisible terrors – a last, safe sound. The twentieth-century mother who seeks to surround her child with a comforting sense of history and rootedness represents him as the earliest icon of innocence. It has been prepared from the beginning of the poem: it comes with the force of recognition, less of surprise. The boldness of the claim keeps the poem open: Mary cradling her son; any mother regarding her sleeping baby; Sylvia Plath watching Nick by candlelight.

This poem of maternal love is one to bear in mind if you are tempted to characterize Plath's work as the poetry of hate and horror. All her capacities were large, and perhaps it is her lack of reticence about them that makes a less demonstrative British audience uneasy. Hughes has put it this way:

> What she was most afraid of was that she might come to live outside her genius for love, which she also equated with courage, or 'guts', to use her word. This genius for love she certainly had, and not in the abstract. She didn't quite know how to manage it: it possessed her. It

fastened her to cups, plants, creatures, vistas, people in a steady ecstasy.[9]

In reading these poems about motherhood, have you found that you agree with the New Critical approach – that we need not know anything more about the author or her times than appears on the page? Or does such knowledge enhance your appreciation? If what she declared she had written about and the poem on the page do not seem identical, is this less a matter of distrusting the author – and trusting the poem – than of finding that the differences increase our insight?

4. Poet as Daughter, or Father as Muse?

To describe Plath's poetry as being 'about' her love/hate relationship with her father would be entirely too reductive, inviting psychoanalytical readings that, however plausible, remain tangential to the finished poems. Nevertheless, this relationship is the dominant theme of many poems. If we say that the death of Otto Plath left his daughter with powerful feelings of loss and resentment, of grief and guilt, and that it affected her subsequent emotional life, then we simply articulate the consequences of parental absence that are psychologically predictable in a general sense. The question that matters is: what do we expect a poet to make of such experience? Do we turn to poetry in the hope that pain and confusion will somehow be rendered meaningful, given a shape which enables us to look steadily at something that threatens to overwhelm us? Do we look to it for articulation of suppressed emotions? And if a specific form of loss is foreign to us, can reading a poem re-create its effect so powerfully that we are able to grasp it, imaginatively? Does a poem, in short, change our way of feeling?

These large questions will recur with particular emphasis when we read 'Daddy', but let's turn first to 'Full Fathom Five' (p. 92). Plath was working on her 'book poems' in the summer of 1958, anxious to have sufficient to submit as a collection for the Yale Series, constantly changing its proposed title. In her journal for 3 July she notes, 'I am rejecting more and more poems from my book, which is now titled after what I consider one of my best and curiously moving poems about my father-sea-god-muse: *Full Fathom Five*'. **What do you think of the poem in comparison with others written around that time – say, 'Battle Scene', or 'Mussel Hunter at Rock Harbour'? Does its imagery connect with any other poems? Does the title's allusion to *The Tempest* give a particular resonance to the poem? Is it anything more than a distancing device? What relation does the speaker have to this father figure? Do you think the poem loses some impetus in the tenth and eleventh stanzas?**

DISCUSSION

The title gives the tonal clue, I think: there is a formality, a 'literariness', a distance from the subject that creates a barrier between the poem and the personal circumstances at its source. Otto Plath was not drowned, of course, but his wilful refusal of a medical diagnosis until it was too late sometimes seemed to Plath a death wish. Remember the figure in 'All the Dead Dears':

> An image looms under the fishpond surface
> Where the daft father went down
> With orange duck-feet winnowing his hair –

which evokes an absurd death by water, robbed of dignity; the narrative voice is tinged with impatience.[1]

This poem's shadow text is *The Tempest*, and Ariel's song:

> Full fathom five thy father lies;
>   Of his bones are coral made:
> Those are pearls that were his eyes:
>   Nothing of him that doth fade,
> But doth suffer a sea-change
> Into something rich and strange.

It falls near the beginning of the play, when Ferdinand believes his father is dead; when they are reunited by the magician Prospero,

Ferdinand exclaims, 'Though the seas threaten, they are merciful.
I have cursed them without cause.'

The old man of the sea in ancient myth is Poseidon or
Neptune, characterized by a tendency towards bad temper and
destructiveness. The sea itself is generally perceived – in psychoanalytical terms, and in literary analysis – as a feminine element,
fluid as opposed to rigid, womb-like, though in this perspective
also capricious and essentially dangerous, liable to overwhelm.
Thus to go down to the sea is to die, but also to be reunited with
the first element, the water that surrounded us before we were
expelled into the air, and thereby to overcome the pain of the
first separation which is birth. The seductiveness of such a death
provides the compelling undertow of this poem, as it does of the
next, 'The Lorelei' (p. 94):

> O river, I see drifting
>
> Deep in your flux of silver
> Those great goddesses of peace.
> Stone, stone, ferry me down there.[2]

There is a strong sense of attraction and repulsion in 'Full
Fathom Five', a tidal ebb and flow of feeling that corresponds not
only to the sea's rhythm but also to that of memory. At the beginning there is no indication of relationship between the speaker and
the subject – 'Old man, you surface seldom' – although 'old man'
is slang for both father and husband. An involuntary movement
produces the sight of the head and spreading hair, the embodiment of 'the old myth of origins / Unimaginable'. The primary
reference, to the beginnings of the human race, is clear enough,
but perhaps there is a secondary sense of the abashed curiosity
individuals have about their own conception – 'unimaginable'.
What the old man represents is 'not to be fathomed', is dangerous
to understand – a nice play on the title, which is taken up again in
the slightly archaic formulation of the following lines. The change
from living to dead is unlike Shakespeare's jewelled transformation, which solidifies the drowned figure into a work of art; here it
becomes insubstantial, dissolves into air. It is like the process of
memory, when figures surface unbidden, will not answer to our
demands and become shadowy when we most want them plain.

The implied contrasts of 'burial' and 'shallow' reinforce this
advance and retreat of meaning. It is such a tightly constructed
poem: 'trench', 'grain' and 'runnel' are all earth words, indwelling, while 'rain', 'channel' and 'ocean' are in this context non-
absorbent, resistant to impression. The face of the sea-god is both
deeply incised by age and yet unaffected by time. Only the next

few lines (stanzas ten and eleven) seem to slip, the deliberation of the metaphor failing to connect with what precedes or follows it – as though Plath liked the word 'durance', and 'the sky's ridgepole', but failed to connect it imaginatively with what she had been building. For the sea as graveyard, with its god rooted among the dead, needs no transitional lines. The old man has no answers that the living may know, and his very presence defies 'other godhood'. There is no room in this vision for a forgiving father, or for a mystery that might encompass charity: anything that is obscure is dangerous, and, despite not being able to look, the poet is magnetized by the danger. The element of seduction is explicit, surely, in 'Your shelled bed I remember'; the speaker is incestuously close to the father, and perversely wishes to return to that state, the perversity apparent in the last line: 'I would breathe water'. The only way to reunite is to die.

What is the effect of the address to the father in the last stanza? If we read the poem as partly written out of a sense of exile from her childhood, presided over by the increasingly with-drawn figure of her father, does this make a difference, give the poem a poignancy that the title and Plath's use of the sea-god myth work to repress?

Clearly one way open to poets concerned to distance themselves from immediate autobiographical sources of poetry, is to utilize a mythical or legendary frame of reference. Yeats's poetry offers a sustained example of this strategy, as does Eliot's *Waste Land*, with its broken but discernible structure of the quest, drawing on medieval narrative of the search for the Holy Grail, and on rituals of death and renewal described in recent anthropological work.[3] Since the late nineteenth century psychologists as well as anthropologists have been intrigued less by specific legends and myths than by the general patterns of social and emotional behav-iour that they embody: the fears and taboos of a culture, part of its deeper structure that can only be articulated figuratively. To use any of these figures, then, is not a kind of decoration, or a disguise, but a way of tapping into a reservoir of meaning.

In the modern period, such figures have often been used by male authors as ironical parallels, or with comic ingenuity as in Joyce's *Ulysses*. Women writers, on the other hand, have tended to be interested less in this form of myth as a commentary which privileges the past and diminishes the present than in discovering or emphasizing continuities and the communal aspects of experi-ence. Adrienne Rich declares, 'Re-vision – the act of looking back and seeing with fresh eyes, of entering an old text from a new critical direction – is for women more than a chapter in cultural history: it is an act of survival.'[4]

This has consequences for language, as Alice Ostriker notes in writing about the 'gaudy and abrasive colloquialism' of poets such as Plath, Anne Sexton and Margaret Atwood. It 'not only modernizes what is ancient, making us see the contemporary relevance of the past. It also reduces the verbal glow that we are trained to associate with mythic material'.[5] Do you think this does apply to Plath's work?

Perseus, Oedipus, the Maenads, Electra – these Greek mythical figures appear in her writing up to *The Colossus* then drop away. In a journal entry for 25 February 1959, Plath declares:

> My main thing now is to start with real things: real emotions, and leave out the baby gods, the old men of the sea, the thin people, the knights, the moon-mothers, the mad maudlins, the Lorelei, the hermits and get into me, Ted, friends, mother and brother and father and family. The real world. Real situations, behind which the great gods play the drama of blood, lust and death. (*Journals*, p. 296)[6]

So the strategies of 'Full Fathom Five' have to be left behind, but there is still a sense of personal drama being played out on a mighty stage: the gods could not be abandoned entirely. As you will see from the notes in the *Collected Poems*, it was at this time that Plath visited her father's grave for the first time: comparing her brief journal entry quoted there with the description of Esther Greenwood's similar visit in *The Bell Jar* and the poem 'Electra on the Azalea Path' (p. 116) is an interesting exercise: please turn to that poem now. **How would you describe the differences between the prose and the poetic versions of this discovery of her father's grave?** The note points out that Plath rejected the poem from her first volume on the grounds that it was 'too forced and rhetorical'. **Would you agree? What makes it so?**

DISCUSSION

'I borrow the stilts of an old tragedy' – the line itself shows awareness of an element of the ridiculous in the poem. Plath pre-empts our possible objection that there is something farcical about her assumption of Electra's role by exploiting that quality quite openly: it is a persistent defence mechanism. 'Masks' is the word we might have expected; 'stilts' reveals the high ambition on shaky foundations. And certainly the language is high-flown, a pastiche of dramatic soliloquy:

> Another kind of redness bothers me:
> *The day your slack sail drank my sister's breath*
> *The flat sea purpled like that evil cloth*
> *My mother unrolled at your last homecoming.*
> I borrow the stilts of an old tragedy.
> The truth is, one late October, at my birth-cry
> A scorpion stung its head, an ill-starred thing;
> My mother dreamed you face down in the sea.

The reference is to Agamemnon, king of Mycenae and leader of the Greek forces in the Trojan War, who could not set sail because of contrary winds. In order that these should change, he obeyed a command to sacrifice his daughter, Iphigenia. There are several versions of the story; in Aeschylus' *Oresteia* she is indeed killed. When Agamemnon returns from Troy his wife, Clytemnestra, kills him in his bath. Their daughter Electra is later reunited with her brother Orestes, and encourages him in the avenging murder of their mother. This chain of deaths questions notions of fate and justice, guilt and responsibility, and in that way answers to some of Plath's preoccupations in her own family relationships. Note, by the way, the persuasively confidential tone in which she addresses the reader, 'The truth is . . .', while offering a further, enigmatic version of the circumstances.

> The stony actors poise and pause for breath.
> I brought my love to bear, and then you died.
> It was the gangrene ate you to the bone
> My mother said; you died like any man.
> How shall I age into that state of mind?
> I am the ghost of an infamous suicide,
> My own blue razor rusting in my throat.
> O pardon the one who knocks for pardon at
> Your gate, father – your hound-bitch, daughter, friend.
> It was my love that did us both to death.

The last line – Electra or Plath? – is a hysterical claim, a statement not borne out by events either mythical or personal, and in that sense is a forced conclusion. Plath did try suicide, knocking at the gate of death behind which lay her father; the blue razor is far more dramatic than a bottle of pills. Yet there is a question that is by no means rhetorical: 'How shall I age into that state of mind?' How is the inevitability of death to be accepted, in any event, and particularly by a child in regard to her parent? This is real grief. It also betrays, perhaps, real resentment.

A flawed poem, yes, but the imagination is working to powerful effect in it. Notice two things: the title itself, and the opening image. Think of that cliché 'X was on the war-path' and see how neatly it has been turned here. (Is it clear that Azalea Path is the name of a cemetery?) We know that Otto Plath wrote about bees; the theme of the next poem, 'The Beekeeper's Daughter', recurs in *Ariel*. Here the matter is not pursued but the choice of the Electra myth is particularly apt, as the royal tombs at Mycenae were in the shape of beehives, and one of the best-known of them is the Tomb of Clytemnestra.

So a turning away from 'baby gods' did not mean that gods entirely disappeared from Plath's work. There was something in their stony, gigantic quality that answered to a poetic need. The title poem of Plath's collection *The Colossus* shows her reconsidering the theme of the lost/buried/drowned father in a manner both more inventive and more sustained than before: let us look at that now (p. 129). The Colossus at Rhodes, one of the Seven Wonders of the ancient world, was a bronze statue of the Greek sun-god supposed to have stood astride the entrance to the harbour, so that ships would sail between its legs. It was in fact 100–115 feet high, and was toppled by an earthquake in 224 BC. **What is it in the poem that identifies it as Sylvia Plath's? Can you see why Plath might describe it as 'colorful and amusing' (*Journals*, p. 325)? And what do the last three lines imply?**

DISCUSSION

The significance of the statue is clear enough: an enormous figure, catastrophically removed from sight and irrecoverable in its original form. It is close to the small child's view of her wondrous parent – and yet, the dignity of this colossal presence is severely compromised in the poem's first stanza: the giant sounds like a barnyard. I think this is the kind of phrase Ostriker had in mind with regard to 'reducing the verbal glow'.

Furthermore, the tone of the next stanza hovers between the lightly accusing and a wearied impatience: 'Perhaps you consider yourself an oracle...'. It is he, not she, who has set himself up as the interpreting voice. But she has colluded, spent all these years clearing his throat. What might this mean in terms of her own use of language?

You might like to look up her story 'Among the Bumblebees' (in *Johnny Panic*), which is very plainly an autobiographical account of the loss of a godlike father; he takes 'Alice' on his back as he swims, and shows her the secrets of bumblebees. The story opens: 'In the beginning there was Alice Denway's father...'; the echo of St John's gospel is deliberate: 'In the beginning was the

Word . . . and the Word was God.' The implications for Plath, and for women writers in general, of this linkage of male authority, godlike power and, as it seems, ownership of the language (although, of course, Mary bore the son of God, that is, the Word), is something that feminist critics have illuminatingly explored. Plath tended to link the father-figure with an oracular figure; let me refer you here to the poem 'On the Decline of Oracles' (p. 78), written in 1958 at the same time as 'The Disquieting Muses', both on paintings by de Chirico. The titles suggest a relationship between the disappearance of the male (and his voice) and the ascendancy of the female in her accusing silence.

Something of the sculptural quality of 'The Colossus' may derive from de Chirico's paintings as much as from the legendary Colossus: his *Enigma of the Oracle* shows on the right a brilliant white head above a dark curtain, much taller than the draped figure on the left, which seems to contemplate a churning sea. Plath wanted to use as epigraph to her earlier poem a quotation from de Chirico: 'Inside a ruined temple the broken statue of a god spoke a mysterious language' (*Journals*, p. 211). So we can see her working and reworking the notion that the dead father had something to say that she cannot grasp, and in both de Chirico's painting and 'On the Decline of Oracles' the message or expectation is related to the sea.

Let us look briefly at the opening of 'On the Decline of Oracles': can you see how Plath's art has developed from this, even in so short a time?

> My father kept a vaulted conch
> By two bronze bookends of ships in sail,
> And as I listened its cold teeth seethed
> With voices of that ambiguous sea
> Old Böcklin missed, who held a shell
> To hear the sea he could not hear.
> What the seashell spoke to his inner ear
> He knew, but no peasants know.

There is no explicit connection, after all, with de Chirico, and the mention of Böcklin seems entirely arbitrary. The poem seems to have begun with an event and then moved into exercise. In the end, the images become portentous, and lose any sense of personal association; they become pieces of a puzzle jammed into place. The first stanzas, however, I suspect arose from information in James Thrall Soby's study of de Chirico, when he discusses Böcklin's influence. A shrouded figure in one of Böcklin's paintings is reproduced in *The Enigma of the Oracle*. The Tuscan peasants, used to Northern painters who revelled in the Italian

landscape, were puzzled by Böcklin's behaviour, as Soby recounts:
'Toward the end of his life, for example, Böcklin had sat for hours
in his garden, paralysed and near death, but holding to his ears
great sea shells so as to hear the roar of an ocean he could no
longer visit.'[7] The landlocked painter's gesture must have had a
peculiar poignancy for Plath, given her association of the loss of
seascape with the loss of her father, but in this early poem she
does not seem to dare to explore its meaning, so that the second
half of the poem is abruptly impersonal. In 'The Colossus', on the
other hand, her associations float freely, and the structure of the
poem is more fluid, less willed.

De Chirico, incidentally, commended Böcklin for exploiting
the 'tragic aspects of statuary': his own use of statues is more dis-
ruptive. The legacy of classical civilization for an early twentieth-
century Italian painter was problematic in the same way as the
legacy of Renaissance literature was for T.S. Eliot. Plath does not
have this sense of responsibility to a tradition (it was not until
she went to Cambridge that she felt its potentially inhibiting
presence), as distinct from an art, nor is she bound by the particularly male aspect of creativity that sculpture in the main represents. In 'The Colossus' it is the particularly female role of
housekeeper that she assumes in relation to this colossal, fallen
figure. Even the word 'gluepot' suggests the inadequacy of resources to the task. Note that word 'tumuli', so typical of the
thesaurus-using Plath; here its precise Latinity seems apt to the
classical setting. (It also reminds me of Magritte's surrealist painting *Napoleon's Death Mask*, a blank-eyed blue head with clouds
floating across it.) Why do you think she evokes the *Oresteia*
here?

> A blue sky out of the Oresteia
> Arches above us. O father, all by yourself
> You are pithy and historical as the Roman Forum.
> I open my lunch on a hill of black cypress.
> Your fluted bones and acanthine hair are littered
>
> In their old anarchy to the horizon-line.
> It would take more than a lightning-stroke
> To create such a ruin.
> Nights, I squat in the cornucopia
> Of your left ear, out of the wind,
>
> Counting the red stars and those of plum-color.

There is a pause for consideration from this industrious,
hopeless, endless work of recovery, as though the speaker could
step back from it all, gaze detachedly on the ruins as she once
had on the Forum. How does the word 'pithy' strike you there?

'Acanthine' hair is both an exact description of sculptured curls which mimic the curved, acanthus-leaf carving above classical columns, and an echo from 'Full Fathom Five', where the sea-god's hair extends for miles.

The strength of Plath's poem, it seems to me, is that it not only concerns the parent–child relationship, rooted in personal circumstance yet sufficiently unspecific here to allow readers to share the disturbance and pain inherent in the process of apparently unending search, but also that it can be interpreted in a wider sense of a culture's lost direction. Without making grandiose claims for the poem, I think that the sense of irreparable damage done by the two world wars in this century – 'more than a lightning-strike' – to an ideal of Western civilization, based on classical foundations, is certainly a presence in the poem. We will return to this matter of Plath's historical imagination.

Working against the 'stony' imagery, the unyielding coldness of the male colossus, are the involuntarily comic noises it emits, and then its fertility and colour by association. 'Cornucopia' gives us an image of the whorled shell of the ear: the horn of plenty in painting spills its fruit, and here we have the surprisingly luscious stars. Is this gesture, sheltering in the remains of something that once sheltered her, a move back into childhood, a terrible admission ('I crawl') of the need for security? We need to judge this in order to know how to read the close of the poem.

'And the long shadows cast by unseen figures – human or of stone it is impossible to tell' – Plath thus described de Chirico (*Journals*, p. 211). 'My hours are married to shadow': her days are given over to effort that makes no impression, the work of 'an ant in mourning'. It is not possible, I think, to see that as a fruitful effort, although one critic has valiantly maintained that the stone figure, while obstructive, is imperfect, and that the last lines should be read as those of a woman who is no longer content to wait.[8] That seems to go against the grain of the poem: the speaker has given up waiting because she no longer hopes for rescue. There is a sense of exhaustion; the woman herself is perhaps only a 'shadow' of her former self. The landing stones are 'blank' of promise; she will not be setting sail.

There is more anguish than anger in 'The Colossus': anger, though, gives a kick-start to 'Daddy' (p. 222). Published in the posthumous collection *Ariel*, it has been one of the poems arousing the fiercest arguments about Plath's poetic standing. Please read this poem now. Some readers have found her voice shrill in 'Daddy', over-insistent and crudely manipulative. Would you

agree? She herself, as the notes point out, declared that 'I' was not
Sylvia Plath at all, but 'a girl with an Electra complex' and mixed
German–Jewish parentage who had to 'act out the awful little
allegory once over' in order to be free of it. (An Electra complex is
the girl's desire for her father and a wish to do away with her
mother, who is a rival in his affections). **Does Plath's statement
make a different to your reading of the poem? Is there a distinction to be made between persona and personality?**

DISCUSSION

However often I read this poem, I am compelled to read it to the
end. It never loses its incantatory power, its nursery-rhyme swing.
You could say it is a kind of proto-rap music. 'And the language
obscene // An engine an engine / Chuffing me off…': is this not
the effect it has on us, too, propelling us towards the defiant
conclusion without a pause for reflection? (Would you say that
Plath was a reflective poet at all?) Even the constant repetitions,
like a stuck record needle, serve to emphasize the drama rather
than slow the action; they make it inescapable. If in 'The
Colossus' the speaker had a housewife's sturdy vigour, cleaning
and mending, here it is a febrile actress's energy, throwing herself
into the part with a manic, total conviction. (It is a metaphor that
Plath exploits to great effect in 'Lady Lazarus'.) And we should
note that it is not only the Jew's skin she imagines herself into, but
an underclass in America as well, 'poor and white' – though that
is also the literal description of the foot emerging from the shoe.
The nursery-rhyme rhythm may remind you of an actual rhyme:
'The Old Woman who lived in a shoe' – it adds a touch of the
laughably bizarre to this telling image. She may have been enclosed in the heavy shoe, and therefore helpless, but if that shoe
was stamping and kicking she was also an involuntary accomplice.
A border line of guilt is difficult to establish.

    Here the 'statuary', far from being tragic, is absurdly
pompous, but it gives way to the one lyrical moment of the poem,
after which 'Ach du' sounds tender, not guttural, with its intimate
form of address. Alvarez has said that the poem, despite everything, is 'a love poem': can you see why? How does 'Daddy' affect
us as a word, as opposed to 'Father', which she has used before?
The note of intimacy anyway is shrugged off in the remorseless,
razing onrush of the poem – why does Plath use 'Polack' not
'Polish' friend here? – to elaborate the metaphors of repression
into their most extreme form: he a Nazi, she a Jew. Even that first
stanza suggests Jews crouched in hiding – Anne Frank in her attic

– scarcely daring to breathe or sneeze. And there are rhymes with 'Jew' throughout the poem, so that even when the word itself is not used its sound is insistently there. 'You' and 'Jew' are bound verbally, inescapably, in a brutal relationship of tyrant and victim.

Furthermore, there are nameless spectres from folklore, the black man who eats children, the vampire with a stake in his heart: the 'pretty red heart' (hearts and flowers are a typically Germanic decorative pattern; indeed, Plath painted them on her children's furnishings), its blood sucked out to fatten the 'black heart' of the suspected murderer.[9] On to the legendary figures Plath grafts her specific experience: 'the Polish town' her own father came from, his profession as a teacher, his death and the cycle of death it inaugurated – a suicide attempt in her twenties. Think of the 'mendings' in 'Stones', and this vengeful reinterpretation:

> But they pulled me out of the sack,
> And they stuck me together with glue.
> And then I knew what to do.
> I made a model of you,
> A man in black with a Meinkampf look
>
> And a love of the rack and the screw.
> And I said, I do, I do.
> So daddy, I'm finally through.

As with the image of the shoe, the frisson here is provided by a sense of the victim's complicity with the torturer. There is an element of sexual thrill in the very act of submission to violence, heightened by the incestuousness of marriage to the father's double – and a desire to give herself to death.

Freud is still providing a model in this poem – the Electra complex – and the self-analysis is done before our eyes, like a conjuring trick: I always wanted to look up to a man; the tougher he treated me the more I liked him (one died, one went away); I married a man just like my father – I've been through all that and now I'm through with those myths of power and torment. Is this reductive simplicity merely for poetic purposes, to create a good show? Or is it more deeply defiant, articulating, with bravado, the truth of women's experience, not just Plath's? Critics in their turn have analysed Plath's procedure in terms of Freudian 'transference', so that her rage over being abandoned is projected on to the enraged father and his sadistic double who deliberately and physically hurt her.

Helen Vendler, in her very perceptive review of the *Collected Poems*, remarks:

This *Threepenny Opera* style is an effect usable only once; the violence done to the self here . . . is the substance of the jeering style. Plath lashes out at her former idolatry of her father and at her subsequent idolatry of her husband, but she also demolishes the noble myths of her own earlier poems, turning the Freudian-Hellenic colossus into 'a ghastly statue with one gray toe/ Big as a Frisco seal'.[10]

The analogy with the 1928 Brecht–Weill opera (you may know at least one song from it, 'Mack the Knife') hits the note exactly: slangy, contemptuous of bourgeois ethics, shockingly witty, violent in places and, of course, German–though pre-Hitlerian. It is a theatrical poem: you could think of it as an operatic aria. Women as the willing victims of male aggressors have a long theatrical history. And as so often in opera, sometimes in the theatre too, the artificiality embarrasses us: this is not 'like life', we think, watching the heroine expire over twenty minutes' singing. Or we allow it as a convention of the form. Kafka suggested that we did not have to make such allowances:

A pupil mocks his teacher who speaks of nothing but death: 'You talk about death all the time but still you don't die.' 'And I'll die all the same, I'm just singing my last song. One man's song is longer, another's shorter. The difference, however, can never be more than a few words.'
    This is true, and it's unjust to smile about the hero who lies mortally wounded on the stage and sings an aria. We lie on the ground and sing for years.[11]

Your conclusion will depend, to some extent, on how you judge the tone of 'I'm through': as defiance – even as an echo of D.H. Lawrence's triumphant line 'Look! We have come through!' – or as exhausted capitulation.

    Readers have tended to concentrate on the German/Jewish metaphor and to say either that its appropriation was fraudulent, devaluing the historical experience, or that the allusions daringly illuminate not only Plath's personal situation but the predicament of women in general, passively accepting their fate (as the Jews seem to have accepted theirs after centuries of persecution), at last giving tongue to the anger of which society has denied the existence.[12] Have you come to one or other of these conclusions yourself? Does the poem provoke you into making a moral judgement on it?

    I should like to step back a little, and look at the literary and historical context of the poem. While it was written in 1962, it was not published in a collection until 1965, after her death. Two events of the early 1960s had given the issue of the Nazi genocide a fresh relevance. One was the capture of Adolf Eichmann in

Argentina in 1960. He was an Austrian Nazi, a member of the SS and one of the chief administrators of the extermination programme. He was taken to Israel and there given an extremely public trial in 1961; Hannah Arendt, reporting on it in *Eichmann in Jerusalem*, came up with her famous formulation 'the banality of evil': the whole murderous process had not been exotic and extraordinary, but had been administered bureaucratically, with attention to train timetables and so forth, and everything was in the records as though they concerned the sale of stamps or tax collection rather than the systematic destruction of peoples. On another, more popular level, was the release of the film *Judgement at Nuremberg* in 1961, in which Spencer Tracy played an American judge presiding over German war-criminal trials. It was an honourable attempt to come to terms with issues of guilt and responsibility in a form that reached millions.

In 1962 Penguin Books published A. Alvarez's anthology *The New Poetry*, which did not include poems by Plath (although his revised edition of 1965 did) because she was not British. The Penguin anthology of contemporary American poetry edited by Donald Hall, also published in 1962, did not include her either, presumably because she lived in England. How much does her nationality influence the way she writes: does it help to see her as an American poet? Peter Orr, interviewing her, suggested somewhat obtusely that 'Daddy' was 'the sort of poem that a real American could not have written, because...these names [Auschwitz, etc.] do not mean so much, on the other side of the Atlantic, do they?' To which Plath replied:

> Well now, you are talking to me as a general American. In particular, my background is, may I say, German and Austrian. On one side I am a first generation American, on one side I'm second generation American, and so my concern with concentration camps and so on is uniquely intense. And then, again, I'm rather a political person as well, so I suppose that's what part of it comes from.[13]

As Alvarez later remarked, Plath's poetry made sense of the terms in which he was discussing British poetry in general. He castigated the latter for its insular 'gentility': 'the belief that life is always more or less orderly, people always more or less polite, their emotions and habits more or less decent and more or less controllable: that God, in short, is more or less good'.[14] This belief, he wrote, had surely been rocked to its foundations not only by the two world wars, but by the specific forms of the Second World War: civilian bombing, and eventually the atom bomb; concentration camps and the Nazi genocide. Moreover, these wars had coincided with the popularity of Freudian psychoanalysis, and a recognition of the way in which forces that are negative at best, evil at worst, are at work within the individual psyche. Of pre-1939 English writers, Alvarez thought that D.H. Lawrence had been the only one able to admit such disturbing forces. (Lawrence, incidentally, was a writer Plath found very congenial; she asks, 'Why do I feel I would have known and loved Lawrence. How many women must feel this and be wrong!' (*Journals*, p. 196).)

The First World War has had a much greater impact on the British literary imagination than the Second. One of the poets whom it has deeply affected is Ted Hughes, who heard his father's stories of trench warfare, and has written out of that personal memory and the collective memory of the culture. Do you think his vision of the continuing 'war between vitality and death'[15] has anything in common with Plath's? Hughes escapes Alvarez's strictures, in fact comes in for his praise: he writes the kind of 'serious' poetry others of his generation did not. And by serious Alvarez did not mean that English poets had to write poems concerned with 'psycholanalysis, or with the concentration camps or with the hydrogen bombs or with any other of the modern horrors'. That would run the risk of propaganda. Writers needed to admit the existence of fears and desires they did not wish to face, and then use all their 'intelligence and skill to make poetic sense of them'.

But were the events of 1939–45 simply on too large a scale and too horrific for poetry to make sense of them? The German philosopher, Theodor W. Adorno, in his rigorous essay 'Cultural Criticism and Society', remarked that 'Even the most extreme consciousness of doom threatens to degenerate into idle chatter. Cultural criticism finds itself faced with the final stage of the dialectic of culture and barbarism. To write poetry after Auschwitz is barbaric.'[16] This attitude was reduced to the formula of 'no poetry after Auschwitz'. The title of George Steiner's influential book *Language and Silence* (1967) echoes such a formulation.

If writers were not to fall silent in the wake of this enormity, they had to deal with the contamination of language that it involved. The distortion of language by totalitarian governments is very much a live issue at the end of the twentieth century; English-language speakers should not feel too complacent, since the euphemisms coined by Western governments have an insidious effect on our own perceptions of events. After 1945, of course, their sullied language was a particular concern for the Germans, and surfaces specifically in 'Daddy', and also in 'Little Fugue' (p. 187):

I see your voice
Black and leafy, as in my childhood,

A yew hedge of orders,
Gothic and barbarous, pure German.

Aurelia Schober, Plath's mother, had spoken German at home
with her parents until an incident at school caused her father to
forbid its use: English was to be the sign of their integration into
American life. Apparently she sang German songs to her children,
and in her journal Plath recalls her mother singing a setting of
Heine's poem, 'Lorelei': 'Ich weiss nicht, was soll es bedeuten...'[17]
She was always urging herself to work at German during her
writing year in America, and wrote to her mother after the session
with the Ouija board that sparked off her own poem 'Lorelei',
that the element of kinship with things German was a new recognition for her (*Letters Home*, p. 346); it sounds a fairly anodyne
matter there. To Germans, at least to those born before 1945,
their country was the 'Fatherland': Plath's father's land was
Germany.[18] You might bear this affinity in mind when reading
'Daddy', and think about what it means in that context.

So let us return to 'Daddy', aware of this mesh of
circumstance – personal, historical and literary-critical. **How does
it change your view of the poem? Do the personal and the historical combine to embody some intuition about the nature of
both?**

Two critics sum up the debate over 'Daddy': please read their
comments and consider your own position. In *Language and
Silence*, George Steiner praises it in the highest terms as:

> One of the very few poems I know of in any language to come near
> the last horror. It achieves the classic art of generalization, translat-
> ing a private, obviously intolerable hurt into a code of plain state-
> ment, of instantaneously public images which concern us all. It is the
> 'Guernica' of modern poetry. And it is both histrionic and in some
> ways 'arty', as is Picasso's outcry.[19]

Seamus Heaney, in his lectures *The Government of the Tongue*,
considers the poet's 'need to get beyond ego in order to become
the voice of more than autobiography', and fails 'Daddy' on these
grounds:

> however brilliant a *tour de force* it can be acknowledged to be, and
> however its violence and vindictiveness can be understood or excused
> in the light of the poet's parental and marital relations, [it] re-
> mains, nevertheless, so entangled in biographical circumstances and
> rampages so permissively in the history of other people's sorrows
> that it simply overdraws its rights to our sympathy.[20]

DISCUSSION

Steiner is himself Jewish; his parents moved from Germany to France, and thence to New York in 1940. The comparison he makes is between 'Daddy' and Picasso's painting commemorating the bombing of a Spanish city by the Fascists during the Spanish Civil War. Steiner finds the combination of raw emotion and artistic control in the poem so powerful that he reasons 'only irresistible need could have brought it off'. But he still avoids the issue: does need justify, validate, the means?

Plath has a temperamental insight into the relationship of authority and passivity/self-hatred that is persuasive. The comparison of herself with the Jews is insidiously present from the outset, although it is almost offhand when it is later articulated: 'I think I may well be a Jew' / 'I may be a bit of a Jew' – and the Jewishness of that stanza is exotic, a part to be shrugged on or off.

In the end it is this element of theatricality, the element of choice, that makes me side with Heaney rather than Steiner, despite the poem's aesthetic excitements. The 6 million Jews who were murdered had no choice: their identity meant death. Plath's identification with their victimization gives her poem the shock value she sought. Whatever psychological compulsions and dramas drove Plath, and even allowed her to express a truth about human relations where they are deformed by masochism and brutality, they were not simply her inalienable birthright. It would have taken, doubtless, an effort of extreme will to turn real pains and disabilities to a different end – in life as in her poetry – but her existence was never perceived as a crime. That, however, was the fate of the Jews of Europe.

5. 'Is there no way out of the mind?'

In 'Apprehensions', Plath gives graphic expression to her sense of being trapped within her own, unrelenting mental space: 'There are no trees or birds in this world, / There is only a sourness.' It is

the world of the bell-jar. Yet there are trees – most persistently,
the yew – and birds in her poems, though they are not consoling presences. When asked about the poems she wrote as an
adolescent, or even earlier, Plath said that they were about

> Nature, I think: birds, bees, spring, fall, all those subjects which are
> absolute gifts to the person who doesn't have any interior experience
> to write about. I think the coming of spring, the stars overhead, the
> first snowfall and so on are absolute gifts for a child, a young poet.[1]

Of course nature and the interior life are not mutually exclusive
subjects. If we go back to the Romantic period, we find Coleridge
exploring their relationship in his *Notebooks*:

> In looking at objects of Nature while I am thinking, as at yonder
> moon glimmering thro' the dewy window-pane, I seem rather to be
> seeking, as it were *asking*, a symbolical language for something
> within me that already and forever exists, than observing anything
> new.[2]

A scene may be internalized so that the 'objective' prospect offered
to the eye – sheep grazing on the West Yorkshire moors, for
example – becomes a projection of the poet's inner life: it yields
terror and apprehension, or a calming pleasure. Consciousness of
nature cannot be arbitrarily separated from a consciousness of
self: at least, this is the Romantic lesson. And brooding beneath
that consciousness is a painful awareness of time: the progress of
the seasons as a reminder of mortality, on the one hand, or the
cycle of birth and decay which is endless, and reduces one person's
lifetime to a tiny element in the ongoing process of nature, on the
other.

Does nature mean something different to American and
European poets? The poems we will be considering here – 'Two
Campers in Cloud Country' (p. 144), 'Watercolour of Granchester
Meadows' (p. 112), 'Wuthering Heights' (p. 167), 'The Moon and
the Yew Tree' (p. 172), 'Poppies in July' (p. 203), 'Winter Trees'
(p. 257) and 'Sheep in Fog' (p. 262) – should be read with this
question in mind. Does a long history of settlement, and of literary
associations, make the English landscape more approachable, less
alienating than the wilderness of America? Or does it mean that
the poet has difficulty in seeing it freshly?

On both sides of the Atlantic, the human relationship to
nature has been complicated in the modern period by immense
changes in the way we live. Despite the fact that most readers now
live far from the landscapes, trees and animals that have been its
traditional sources, nature poetry – loosely speaking, a poetry
of description – is exceptionally persistent. Part of its appeal is
exactly this recreation of a vanished world, and in Britain espec-

ially it is intimately related to a historical landscape which is part of the island's image of itself.

We can trace an English poetic line from Thomas Hardy through Edward Thomas – whose reaction to the First World War was to delineate those continuities that nature represented in a dissolving world – to Philip Larkin, who also instinctively infuses the rural English landscape with nostalgia. When these poets write about animals and birds, it is very much in a human context, often as symbols of a particular order. D.H. Lawrence, on the other hand, resisted anthropomorphism as a form of human conceit. He had a marvellous eye for details of animal behaviour, but his non-domestic creatures are independent, and express themselves in ways that do not necessarily comply with general human notions of how they should look or behave. We do see things differently, reading 'Snake' or 'Baby Tortoise', cajoled by Lawrence's direct tone of address. Lawrence's prose, too, offers a model for the interlocking of physical description with a state of mind – the horses at the end of *The Rainbow*, for example, providing an image for the uncontrollable psyche, a typically Lawrentian desire for and fear of overwhelming.

For Ted Hughes, even more than for Lawrence, the presences in nature are unlikely to console the human spectator, let alone transcend him. They hold up a mirror to human violence, predatoriness, murderous instincts. Yet a return to nature is also presented as a return to energy and instinct that has been overlaid by centuries of 'civilization', a word many modern writers use with profound ambivalence. It is this process of revitalization that Hughes has in mind when he writes about landscape poems in *Poetry in the Making*: a human longing to re-establish contact with something that existed before the strains of civilization: 'we still need occasional holidays back in the old surroundings. . . . It is almost at though these places were generators where we can re-charge our run-down batteries'.[3] Despite his almost holiday-brochure language here, Hughes is talking about places without architectural significance, without specific human associations – not 'Brontë country' as it might be packaged for us today, but real, wild places of the sort that Plath wrote about in 'Two Campers in Cloud Country':

> It is comfortable, for a change, to mean so little.
> These rocks offer no purchase to herbage or people:
>
> They are conceiving a dynasty of perfect cold.
> In a month we'll wonder what plates and forks are for.

The word 'comfortable' here is striking: it is defined metaphysically rather than physically, since the landscape rejects our

domestic definitions of comfort. Yet metaphysics are not necessarily reassuring: in the search for 'old surroundings', we may lose
our sense of ourselves altogether.

That sense of nostalgia works in different ways. It could
have been a trap for Plath, as an Anglophile American: she had
her criticisms – from the absence of efficient home appliances
to the cliquishness of English literary society – but she found
it possible to live a somewhat less conventional life in England
than the pressures of American society seemed to allow. She wrote
at least one *New Yorker*-type poem on an English landscape,
accepted for publication by that most Anglophile of magazines:
'Watercolour of Grantchester Meadows'. 'It is a country on a
nursery plate': the last line tries to indicate that there might be
less attractive things going on in the natural world than the 'mild
air' of the poem suggests: do you think it succeeds? Do you find it
a pleasing poem?

'Wuthering Heights' offers an altogether different experience.
It is less a case of casting off the civilized exterior in order to
discover hidden resources than of having the exterior stripped
away, willy-nilly, leaving no resources at all. For most readers the
poem's title will be inextricably linked with Emily Brontë's novel.
**Does the poem rest on that association at all? What is the import
of the fourth stanza?**

DISCUSSION

Certainly the moors in 'Wuthering Heights' hold out promises
they do not fulfil: the promise of warmth, the hint of colour,
dissolve on approach. The thrust of the opening is cinematic: a
wide shot – the horizons – that then focuses in on the solitary
figure, ringed. It is reminiscent, too, of a Hardy novel. In this
treeless landscape she is marked out as contrary. As in 'Hardcastle
Crags' (p. 62), the weight of the inhuman is 'Enough to snuff the
quick / Of her small heat out', here she can feel the wind 'trying to
funnel my heat away'. Does it make a difference that the earlier
poem is in the third person, and this in the first?

The inscrutable sheep are happier, they at least are at home.
The speaker can establish no connection with them: the possibility
of communing with nature is lost.

> The sheep know where they are,
> Browsing in their dirty wool-clouds,
> Gray as the weather.
> The black slots of their pupils take me in.
> It is like being mailed into space,
> A thin, silly message.

Even if they are described with wry humour, the poet's insubstantiality is what dominates the stanza. She has become thin and flat, always distasteful dimensions for Plath. Like the lintel and sill in the next stanza, she has become unhinged.

Hughes reprinted the poem in *Poetry in the Making*, and remarked that it was not descriptive of the moors themselves, 'but of what it feels like to be walking over them'. As a tall figure, Plath is distressingly obtrusive. She had used the same image in a poem earlier that year, 'I Am Vertical' (p. 162); please read that now for comparison.

> But I would rather be horizontal. . . .
> Compared with me, a tree is immortal
> And a flower-head not tall, but more startling,
> And I want the one's longevity and the other's daring.

(After that fine first stanza, I find that the second declines into self-pity – would you agree? Perhaps it is surprising that Plath does not succumb to it more often).

In 'Wuthering Heights' we have an example of Coleridge's 'symbolical language' in her description of the grass and the valley lights: something in Plath is distracted, delicate, terrified, but the poet does not lose hold of the power to observe existing phenomena in ways that make them seem new to us. Do you think the 'small change' is reductive, purely, or somehow comforting in its domesticity?

Yorkshire is also, however, Hughes's native heath, and I wonder whether that feeling of alienation from the landscape is not generated in part by Plath's knowing that it was his territory, in poetic as well as ancestral terms. Their work stems from two separate traditions of nature poetry. The American, in the tradition of Ralph Waldo Emerson, Walt Whitman, and Wallace Stevens in this century, sees the poet's task as integrating himself with his field of perception, using the ordering imagination. The English, typically empirical, sees the natural world as existing independent of the poet's imagining; perceives civilization, rather than the self, as threatened by irrational forces. W.H. Auden, in his introductory essay to the *Faber Book of Modern American Verse* (1956), discourses on the distinctive imprints of British and American poets: not only are their pace and pitch quite different, but so are their attitudes to nature. For the one it was mythologized, humanized, local and mostly lovable; for the other, 'neither the size nor the condition nor the climate of the country encourages such intimacy'. 'Of real desert, of a loneliness which knows of no enduring relationships to cherish or reject, [the

British] have no conception.'[4] Out of this fundamental environ-
mental and historical difference, Auden maintains, arises their
conceptions of poetry and poets: on the European side a conviction of historical succession, of a literary brotherhood, writing
taken for granted as an art; on the American side 'it is up to each
individual poet to justify his existence by offering a unique product'; Auden is struck by 'how utterly unlike each other' the best
American poets are.

You may recall the remark by Elizabeth Hardwick, quoted in
the introduction, to the effect that Plath's imagery was not drawn
from the local but was psychological. She goes on to say that Plath

> is hard to connect with Massachusetts and New England. There is
> nothing Yankee in her. So 'crossing the water' was easy – she was as
> alien to nostalgia and sentiment as she was to the country itself. A
> basic and fundamental displacement played its part.[5]

It is particularly noticeable to British readers that her sense of
history is not grounded in place, that she has no familial sense of
where she lives – unsurprisingly, since she lived apart from her
family and was occupied in creating her own out of nowhere, in a
way. This lack of rootedness was both a stimulus and a real loss:
it left her landscapes wide open to archetype and symbol, and
correspondingly, it did nothing to shore up her already fragile
identity. Even if she had wanted to kick against it, that would
have given a negative definition. As it is, if you look down the list
of poem titles after 1959, you will see few that indicate specific
location. Without this specificity, the landscapes become more
amenable to the poet's interpretation: we are told how to read
their signs, and have less room to resist the telling. For critics who
believe that the text exists with no outside referent beyond the
reader's mind, the idea that a poem can be 'tested' against reality
has no meaning. Nevertheless, there is a long tradition of verse in
English that rests on quasi-photographic veracity, landscapes that
are both symbolic and palpably real – Eliot's 'Little Gidding' is
just one example. The name is talismanic, the poet wishes to
memorialize the place and what it stands for, not an impulse Plath
shares.

A brilliant example of 'psychological landscape' is her poem 'The
Moon and the Yew Tree' (p. 172), which I think is one of the
finest poems in *Ariel*. Hughes said that he set the subject as an
exercise, and that Plath declared the finished poem to be just that;
he was intensely depressed by it.[6] Please read 'The Moon and the
Yew Tree' now. **Plath has come a long way from writing with a**

thesaurus on her knee: is there any word that calls attention to
itself? What does Plath mean by writing 'the moon is no door' and
'the moon is my mother'? Does the poem have a religious theme?

DISCUSSION

It is a poem full of flat statements, and the distress in it is kept at a
chill level. The colours of the poem – black and blue – are the
colours of a bruised perception: the way the poet sees, we are
persuaded, is the way things really are. We do not expect an
onomatopoeic word like 'bong' in such a serious, adult poem. The
word 'soberly' in front of it forestalls any impulse to smile.

The poem is organized on a very basic visual pattern: the
upright (male) shape of the yew, the round (female) shape of
the moon. These ancient opposites are not in any fruitful
juxtaposition. Poetry, Plath stated, was 'a tyrannical discipline,
you've got to go so far, so fast, in such a small space that you've
just got to turn away all the peripherals'.[7] In commenting on 'The
Moon and the Yew Tree' in her BBC broadcast (see the notes
to the *Collected Poems*), she complained of just this tyranny
with regard to the yew tree itself, which 'began, with astounding
egotism, to manage and order the whole affair'. Does her phrase
'tender melancholy' (an atmosphere superseded by the yew tree's
activity) bear any relation to the poem as it finally emerged?
Does the yew tree in fact dominate the poem to the extent Plath
claimed?

Perhaps the egotism of the yew, in an exercise suggested by
Hughes, was in some way representative of the male authority
Plath both resented and seemed to need. Her own flicker of authority in the first stanza, stepping amidst the wet grasses, is blocked
off by the headstones and an admission of defeated direction.[8]
You might like to compare this stanza with 'Letter in November'
(p. 253): 'And the wall of old corpses. / I love them. / I love them
like history' – what do they share with history?

A concordance to Plath's poetry lists sixty-one references to
the moon[9] and none of them is benevolent. The O-mouth recurs
three times:

> If the moon smiled, she would resemble you.
> You leave the same impression
> Of something beautiful, but annihilating.
> Both of you are great light borrowers.
> Her O-mouth grieves at the world, yours is unaffected...
>   ('The Rival', p. 166)

S. Plath

(1)

Moon + Yew

This is the light of the mind, cold + planetary.
The trees of the mind are black. The light is blue.
The grasses unload their griefs on my feet as if I were god.
~~They~~ prickling my ankles + murmuring of their humility.
Fumey spiritous mists inhabit this place,
Separated from my house by a row of headstones.
I simply cannot see where there is to get to.
The moon is no door. It is a face in its own right,
White as a knuckle, + terribly upset.
It drags the sea after it like a dark crime; it is quiet
~~Full of knees + cold pinnacles~~
With the O-gape of complete despair. I live here.
Twice on sunday, the bells startle the sky.
~~Their metal tongues~~
Eight great tongues affirming the resurrection.
At the end, they soberly bong out their names.

~~The yew points + gradations go on~~
The yew points up. It has a gothic shape.
The eyes lift after it and find the moon.
The moon is my mother, She is not sweet like mary.
Her blue garments unloose small bats + owls.
How I would ~~like~~ to believe in tenderness! —
The face of the effigy, gentled by candles,
Bending, on me in particular, ~~its mild eyes~~
The yew tree is black as a grave, I could step through it
And ~~find myself out the skin in the fairy tale~~
~~In the semi-precious stones + the eyes of dead men.~~
And find myself in a little, airless sack.
~~The dead will have such work to do, gathering their crowns~~
The rector is kind + grey, his ears stick out.
He stands in the way of the gods like a local pebble.
Influences are passing between the stars.
They transfix me, like the arrows of Sebastian.
O the tiny gold lives of divinity, in the old
                                        In an
                                        paintings.

Draft page of 'The Moon and the Yew Tree'

The moon is no door. It is a face in its own right,
White as a knuckle and terribly upset.
It drags the sea after it like a dark crime; it is quiet
With the O-gape of complete despair. I live here.

('The Moon and the Yew Tree')

I feel it enter me, cold, alien, like an instrument.
And that mad, hard face at the end of it, that O-mouth
Open in its gape of perpetual grieving.
It is she that drags the blood-black sea around
Month after month, with its voices of failure.

(*Three Women*, p. 182)

The moon and the mouth (in its various forms – plural, possessive
– mentioned about the same number of times) are identical, and
given to destruction. The image is intensified over the poems, so
that while in the first its beauty is allowed, and grief may even
leave room for tenderness, in the second it has subsided into pure
distress and by the third it is actively hurtful. That particular
complex of female imagery in *Three Women* subverts traditional
associations: the waxing and waning, the connection with the
menstrual cycle and thus with fertility and barrenness – these are
not surprising, but the clinical light itself as an instrument, like a
gynaecological probe, is a frightening transference. This second
voice, of the woman who miscarries, refers again and again to
whiteness and flatness – as opposed to the healthy redness and
roundness of generation – so that the moon is bound up with
what she sees as her failure.

This knot of associations formed by trees, whiteness, moons
and menstruation is pulled tightest in 'The Munich Mannequins'
(p. 262):

Perfection is terrible, it cannot have children.
Cold as snow breath, it tamps the womb

Where the yew trees blow like hydras,
The tree of life and the tree of life

Unloosing their moons, month after month, to no purpose.

Here the yew tree and the moon have lost their existence as real
objects to become symbolic shapes – grotesque in this context – of
plasticity and movement versus unyielding repetition.

In 'The Moon and the Yew Tree' the mimetic O-gape of the
moon, it has been suggested, is implicitly contrasted with the A-
gape – the Greek word for love, used for the love-feast of the
Christians – that characterizes, or should characterize, the church.
Although so much points to the church, the speaker lives outside it
– lives, indeed, in despair. The promise of the Resurrection, the

bells who have their own names – these cannot save her.[10] The Gothic shape of the yew, which should set the soul – like the eye – on its course heavenward, is counteracted by the maternal shape of the moon. The moon's robes of night, blue garments like those of Mary, 'unloose bats and owls'. These creatures may have been sweetened for us by the anthropomorphism of childhood books, but Plath knows that their night flights are predatory expeditions, nothing of mildness there.

'I have fallen a long way': this last stanza, for all its lyricism, paints a cold picture of any alternative to the night out of doors. We say that people 'fall from grace'; the stars, clouds and saints' statues here are graceful in depiction, but that only measures the speaker's distance from them. They are also 'stiff with holiness': nothing unbends towards the speaker, nothing embraces her; she seems to be beyond the reach of God or Mary. The moon is 'bald and wild' – remember the disquieting muses with their 'heads like darning-eggs' – and bereft of maternal feeling, of nuturing. So only the message of the yew, traditionally associated with death, remains constant.

For comparison, turn now to 'Elm' (p. 192), where the tree itself speaks out of the same grid of associations. **What is the effect of the three-line stanza, with its one variable long line, compared with the seven-line stanza of 'The Moon and the Yew Tree'? Have a look at the fragment that Hughes reprints in the notes: can you analyse what happens to the germ of the poem in the printed version?**

DISCUSSION

The colours now are white and red, but here is the tree again, the moon – indifferent, mocking sterility – and the soft flying things that the night releases. Now the voice is 'terribly upset'. Hughes notes that there was a giant wych-elm shadowing their house in Devon. That scarcely matters – Plath is not interested in its geographical situation but in how it speaks to her condition, or of her condition: 'How your bad dreams possess and endow me'. The elm suggests that it might remind her 'of the voice of nothing, that was your madness' – Plath always feared that to stop writing would be fatal.

In the fragment, the tree is described from the outside, in very plain language, with one metaphor: the tree has a heart and a nervous system. The finished poem gives voice to the tree's own perceptions of natural phenomena; it also mocks its abandoned interlocutor – 'Love is a shadow. / How you lie and cry after it.' The draft seems to summarize the narrative of 'The Moon and the Yew Tree', unexcitedly, while the poem's voice is intensely agitated, and the original centre 'very still with wisdom' has become 'incapable of more knowledge'.[11]

At about the same time that Plath wrote 'The Moon and the Yew Tree', Hughes wrote 'Full Moon and Little Frieda'.

> Cows are going home in the lane there, looping the hedges with their
>   warm wreaths of breath—
> A dark river of blood, many boulders,
> Balancing unspilled milk.
>
> 'Moon!' you cry suddenly, 'Moon! Moon!'
>
> The moon has stepped back like an artist amazed at a work
>
> That points at him amazed.

The relaxed humour of the poem (this is its second half), and its equally relaxed syntax – long lines and spaces, a poem for speaking aloud – could scarcely be further from Plath's dissociated fear. The moon, you will have noticed, is male here and like the male poet, an artist. Even that 'dark river of blood' in this context does not seem foreboding – though it might seem Lawrentian. Perhaps you will know the scene in *The Rainbow* when Tom Brangwen takes his little stepdaughter to feed the cows while her mother is in labour, a scene like a genre painting, suffused with tenderness. There's tenderness in the title 'Little Frieda'; do we need to know that she is the poet's daughter? (She has the same name, incidentally, as Lawrence's wife.) It is interesting to me that Hughes has chosen to preserve a moment when the child talks, when she has an intuition that has nothing to do with their relationship, whereas Plath writes about her children (but only her son by name) in their pre-verbal stage, when the element of separation, of individual vision, is not marked. The last lines are humorously observed, yet convey the astonished pleasure of the pointing child, naming and thus inventing her world. They restore an uncomplicated sense of wonder.

Wonder has always been a human response to nature. We look at documentaries on television and are amazed by the intricacies of the social organization of the insect world, or the subtle gradations of colour in fish or bird, and what purpose they seem to serve. We observe landscapes of astounding grandeur – the Scottish highlands, the canyons of Arizona – and yield to that experience of wonder independently of whatever may be going on in our lives. The reaction seems to be pure, like Frieda's to the moon. This is why the Romantics, and many others since, have felt that nature had a healing quality, by allowing absorption in the non-self.

What happens to this impulse, then, when the spectator is emotionally disturbed? The speakers of the poems in *Ariel* often address the subject of madness, when reactions spin out of control. In a suggestive essay, using Plath's 'Poppies in July' as one of his examples, Robert Pinsky explores this matter of wonder and derangement.

> As in the ordinary phrase, wonder takes the distressed personality 'out of himself.' Or, does it take the distress out, putting it into the object of wonder? Such questions may be dealt with by the sensible, conservative idea of 'objectivity.' . . . that idea involves the use of objective natural reality to clarify a difficult state of mind.[12]

Let us look at 'Poppies in July' (p. 203), and also bear in mind 'Poppies in October' (p. 240), with regard to the depiction of natural reality and its impact on a 'difficult state of mind'. You might think about the conventional idea of flowers in poetry, and how radically these differ. **Do poppies have particular associations, and if so, how does Plath exploit them? Is the language of the two poems similar? Do you find that their syntax creates ambiguities of meaning?**

DISCUSSION

In her interview with Peter Orr, Plath mentioned that she was 'very interested in battles, in wars, in Gallipoli, the First World War and so on' – and for British readers the juxtaposition of poppies and July is surely still associated with the First World War, and the scarlet poppies made famous in poetry, picked out for their persistence in flowering with the man-made hell of trench warfare all around them (July being the month of the infamous Somme slaughter in 1916). They are the flowers of Remembrance Day, for all wars. These ones in the peaceable cornfields or grass verges of Devon are so uncannily vivid that the poet cannot help wondering whether they are actually harmful.

But she clearly distinguishes between their existence in nature and in her mind: 'I put my hands among the flames. Nothing burns'. She can describe them with perfect exactitude, by simile – 'like the skin of a mouth' – which then slides into statement – 'little bloody skirts!' The whole process of the analogizing mind has been suppressed, but the exclamation gives us the glee of the

mind in finding the just analogy – 'I know what they look like –
little bloody skirts!' Their shape is skirt-like, as you will know: the
nipped-in waistline blooming out to a full hemline, yet that stain
disturbs us. 'Little red skirts' would have been intolerably banal;
'bloody' transforms the perception. It may be that the association
with war is only secondary to Plath's imagination; she could be
thinking of the onset of puberty and the stain of menstrual blood.

Then there is a change. Poppies are traditionally associated
with sleep and oblivion, with a mock death, something desired.
Keats's luscious 'To Autumn' pictures the season itself 'on a half
reap'd furrow sound asleep, / Drows'd with the fume of poppies'.
So the mouth exhales its fumes of unconsciousness, a rest from the
restless consciousness of the poet's absorbed imagination, yet
Plath knows that what tranquilizes can also sicken. She has an
entirely modern perception of 'nauseous capsules'.

'If my mouth could marry a hurt like that!' What does this
exclamation mean? The poet has already said that poppies do no
harm – they do not burn, they do not drug. They exist independently of her and of the hurt in her own mind. We could say that
the 'derangement' was in that identification of flowers with her
own pain, moreover in the wish to be wedded to the pain (shades
of 'Daddy'?). But the object persists beyond the glass capsule
(again, that bell-jar image) in which the poet is enclosed. 'But
colorless. Colorless'. What is colourless, and why?

Plath's language in this poem, as in 'Poppies in October', is
traditional. Pinsky suggests that her 'language cannot be experi-
mental, we are tempted to say, because the experience and the
emotions are'.[13] It is as though she doggedly fixes something in
place with plain words because all around her things slip away.

> O my God, what am I
> That these late mouths should cry open
> In a forest of frost, in a dawn of cornflowers.

What is Plath saying at the end of 'Poppies in October': that their
flames amidst the blue and white are like some belated revelation,
which she is privileged to witness? Are the poppies a symbol of a
sexual vitality, or perhaps of a sexual wound, while all around the
frost of emotional winter has set in? What relation do they bear to
the woman in the ambulance, and what relation does the poet?
If the penultimate line were punctuated 'cry, / open in a forest' –
as the irregularly rhymed line endings nudge it in that direction –
would it mean something different than it means here? Is there a
deliberate ambiguity?

The residual 'sanity', I think, lies in Plath's recognition that the hurt and the flowers, as much as one might stir the other, are separate things. But she cannot take the further step into finding that consoling: they do not offer 'a way out of the mind'.

Plath's poems of description are rarely concerned with animals – nature red in tooth and claw; the vegetable world seemed to fascinate her. It is certainly not an orderly world of ladylike gardening; indeed, it tends towards the robustly disordered. There is something perhaps in the ecomony of plants that attracts her: nothing goes to waste; what dies serves to regenerate; nothing exists in isolation. The conventional notion that flowers are delicate and fade quickly has often been the basis for comparing them with young women. Feminist critics have suggested that women poets are re-evaluating such imagery, and using it in a way that changes our perception: energy, rather than beauty, force, rather than frailty characterizes it, and mortality becomes simply part of the organic process to which women are closely attuned. I confess that I am wary of arguments which present poetry as biologically determined, even in this positive sense – although no one can deny that gender plays a very large part in our vision of the world.

The argument that women have a special relationship with nature – that they even *are* nature, in a sense – has been used, historically, in a derogatory or patronizing way. If women were closer to nature because of their physiology, their social role (that is, their nurture of children), and their psychic structure then, it was argued, men were closer to culture, and tended to be the creators of culture in its highest sense – art, law, philosophy, institutions. Women, it was said, were rooted in the world as given, while men transcended that world and, lacking a natural outlet for their creative instincts, endeavoured to transform what was given. This nature–culture scale or opposition is elegantly set out in Sherry B. Ortner's essay, 'Is Female to Male as Nature Is to Culture?', where it is exposed as socially or culturally defined rather than biologically inherent (and thus irrefutable, as its proponents had implied). Feminist critics, in redefining the debate, have interpreted it positively. Alice Ostriker, for example, suggests that contemporary women poets are constructing a new myth of nature which does not rely on the accepted consciousness/ naturalness ratio, that is, the more conscious you are, the less natural you can be. They invoke an alliance with nature that is easily available to women writers: 'we are nature with a concept of nature'.[14]

This is a seductive formulation: will it work for Plath? Let us turn to 'Winter Trees' (p. 257).

DISCUSSION

What begins in uncertainty – dissolving contours, symbolizing the way boundaries blur too in human relationships ('a series of weddings') – proceeds to a bitter certainty. The image of the tree as a living record of human history, celebrating beginnings and potential, is abruptly altered by the perspective from which it is viewed. Plath does not love her own kind, and presents their behaviour as plainly inimical to nature – nature, indeed, is ignorant of such behaviour. But even this personal animus flickers suddenly and then dissolves.

Why are the winds 'footless'? She has a gift for teasing the eye and expectation: we might have expected 'footloose', but 'footless'? Why does she say the trees are 'Ledas'? Far from being 'embedded' in nature, the natural is disembodied (footless, otherworldly, shadowy) or denied. What is the effect of that long last line?

Helen Vendler remarks that the way the line is bound by the repetition of words of two syllables is a familiar poetic device.

> But what is more unusual is the matching of 'nothing,' though it is not syntactically parallel, with 'chanting', and 'easing.' Such ear-rhymes are a true binding and a false binding at once, setting the words aslant. The last half of the word 'shadows' – '-dows' – almost matches the 'doves' of 'ringdoves' in the same witty way.... her eye-rhymes continue vigorously to the end of her career, and replace her earlier, self-conscious overwriting for the ear.[15]

The poem, which may seem arbitrary in its associations, moves in a circle, from tree rings to ringdoves: the binding elements are not rigid, however, they fade in and out.

The sense of dissolution is overpowering in 'Sheep in Fog' (p. 262). Plath's description of the background to the poem (p. 295) explains a title that otherwise seems to have little bearing on what follows. Each stanza of the fog-bound poem concerns disappearance or absence: the hills vanishing, breath, rust (iron breaking down), blackening, melting; the heaven without stars (already disappointed) or a father. Completing this poem on 28 January, Plath wrote 'Child' (p. 265) the same day, and there sees her child or child's eye as a reflecting pool that gives back her own image

>   this troublous
> Wringing of hands, this dark
> Ceiling without a star

– 'Starless and fatherless, a dark water'. The self as merely a gesture of anguish, on the edge of darkness: it cannot be written about in such a self-effacing way without bearing witness to a self that is so far diminished as to verge on non-existence. The world is reduced to water, for Plath always the dangerously seductive element.

What does 'nature' mean to Plath in these late poems? It seems to offer a judgement on human behaviour – it is sturdily productive, it is disappointed in her – but nothing to hold on to, nothing to identify with; it 'threatens a heaven'. You might like to read 'Among the Narcissi' (p. 190) and 'Pheasant' (p. 191) to see whether they present exceptions to the general tendency. Think back to the dissolving horizons of 'Wuthering Heights'. If we return to Coleridge's notion that the poet may be looking for a 'symbolical idea of something that exists within' him or her, these images of violence and dissolution in nature are a very disturbing symbol of the self, and profoundly alienating. Despite her gender, Plath cannot ultimately console herself with a cyclical, renewing vision of nature as process, with which she is at one. Oblivion and obliteration are what she sees, and what she seeks.

6. Self-Portraits

How shall I come into the right, rich full-fruited world of middle age? Unless I work . . . Forget myself, myself. Become a vehicle of the world, a tongue, a voice. Abandon my ego . . . (16 September 1959; *Journals*, p. 312)

I shall perish if I can write about no one but myself. . . . Writing is my health; if I could once break through my cold self-consciousness and enjoy things for their own sake, not for what presents and acclaim I may receive. (4 November 1959; *Journals*, p. 325)

I feel it is extreme (and perhaps unique, even) about America, that the artist's existence becomes his art. He is re-born in it, and he hardly exists without it. . . . That would seem embarrassing to an

Englishman, and inhuman, probably, to be that 'all out' about it.
(Robert Lowell)[1]

In Chapter 1, I touched on the matter of confessional poetry, and
asked you to read 'Fever 103°' as an example of that genre as
defined by M.L. Rosenthal. Now I want to return to the problems
posed by making the self, especially a self marked by the experience of mental breakdown, the centre of poetry. Can the 'I' of
such poems be confidently identified with the author? Does
such poetry rely for its effect on some degree of biographical
knowledge?

   The inextricable linkage of self and art described by Lowell
poses particular difficulties for women, intermittently acknowl-
edged by Plath. It has not escaped the notice of her critics that
Plath's father was the writer, her mother the note-taker and
amanuensis; the language of the male was authoritative, of the
female imitative. If societal pressure, backed by maternal instincts
and necessities, has confirmed women's roles as nurturing, sup-
portive and self-effacing, then letting the demanding ego take
centre stage goes against all their training, and has undoubtedly
been an inhibiting factor in the potentially creative lives of many
women. 'Modesty' continues to be a term of praise for women
writers: Anne Stevenson describes Elizabeth Bishop as 'modest
and . . . dignified'; W.H. Auden commended Adrienne Rich's early
poems for being 'neatly and modestly dressed'; oddly enough,
even when finding Plath heroic, Lowell singles out 'her hand of
metal with its *modest*, womanish touch'.[2] Although Plath was
radically uncertain of her identity, by the 1960s there is no sense
that the self was an inappropriate subject for poetic exploration: it
did not have to be 'nice', let alone – as Adrienne Rich described
the much admired Marianne Moore – 'maidenly, elegant, intellectual, discreet'.[3]

   T.S. Eliot famously declared that 'the more perfect the artist
the more completely separate in him will be the man who suffers and the mind which creates': this doctrine of impersonality
strongly influenced his poetic generation, and indeed the younger
Lowell, pupil of these poets. The New Criticism (see Chapter 2)
was equally committed to this notion of restraint: it valued form,
wit, irony – in brief, evidence of intellect rather than emotion
in art. And because this tradition emphasized control, it was
naturally hostile to egoistic biography, for which Eliot had cen-
sored the Romantic poets.

   Plath, who had absorbed such ideas through her university
years and the poetry published in journals, suggested that her own

poetry be read as combining such virtues – above all, the controlling intelligence – with the freedom to express formerly taboo emotion:

> I think my poems immediately come out of the sensuous and emotional experiences I have, but I must say I cannot sympathize with these cries from the heart that are informed by nothing except a needle or a knife, or whatever it is. I believe that one should be able to control and manipulate experiences, even the most terrifying, like madness, being tortured... with an informed and an intelligent mind. I think that personal experience is very important, but certainly it shouldn't be a kind of shut-box and mirror-looking, narcissistic experience.[4]

How does this background and Plath's statement square with your reading of her poetry? Would the latter stand as a definition or 'confessional' for her work? Is her manipulation of extreme experiences what makes it compelling?

Let us turn to 'Parliament Hill Fields' (p. 152), a poem about an intensely personal loss. In his early paper 'Mourning and Melancholia', which Plath herself seized on as 'an almost exact description of my feelings and reasons for suicide' (*Journals*, p. 279), Freud suggested that while both emotional states were related to the loss of a loved object, someone suffering from melancholia might 'know *whom* he has lost, but not *what* has been lost in him'. Whereas a person in mourning sees the outside world as poor and empty, Freud thought that in melancholia this perception was transferred to the ego, the self. The mourner feels remorseful, and reproaches herself, but also tries to repress these feelings; the melancholic is almost the opposite, and according to Freud displays a 'trait of insistent communicativeness which finds its satisfaction in self-exposure'.[5] If we adopt Freud's distinction, how would you characterize this poem?

Plath's introduction to it for a BBC reading (pp. 290–1) summarizes its movement: from blankness to convalescence, to a sense of residual vitality, implying recovery. Is this true to your reading of the poem? If we did not have the note, how clear would it be that the poem concerned a miscarriage? Would it make a difference to our reading if the 'I' of the poem and Plath were not the same person? Does the formal organization of the poem in any way contradict or undermine the overt emotion expressed in it?

DISCUSSION

Unlike 'Daddy', 'Parliament Hill Fields' is not concerned with a psychological family drama, yet the event at its heart and the speaker's peculiar relationship to it – 'Your absence is inconspicuous; / Nobody can tell what I lack' – brings before the reader a private grief in an act of public mourning. The death of her father was something with which, despite the defiance of 'Daddy', Plath never seems to have come to terms, and she had to work over and over that loss, testing the boundaries of its meaning. According to the Freudian model, 'Parliament Hill Fields' can be seen as a poem of mourning, as opposed to the poems of 'melancholia' – like 'Daddy' – dominating Plath's *oeuvre*. In this poem Plath is able to explore a loss of whose meaning she is fully conscious. Six days before the poem was written, she had a miscarriage.

While she mentions 'a speaker' and 'a woman' in her introduction, there is no sense that Plath is distancing herself from the experience she describes; it seems to me a fully autobiographical 'I'. Yet the tone of the 'I' is uninsistent, calls little attention to itself, and in that way is untypical of the confessional mode. Although the title specifies a location in London, the poem does not rely on that for its resonance: there is no sense of Plath's personal connection with the place. Her anonymity makes the experience almost archetypal. The whole landscape is made to speak of loss, the inconspicuous in that way being made visible.

Within that landscape, the speaker – paradoxically – is merely 'a stone, a stick', something that has no holding power, offers no resistance. Have you noticed similar imagery in other poems by Plath? It is constantly associated with illness: here, by association – the gulls flutter 'like the hands of an invalid', 'The wind stops my breath like a bandage.' This silent, unresponsive, almost invisible being – 'Ghost of a leaf, ghost of a bird' – thus takes on the qualities of the foetus. The poem concerns the process of letting go, saying goodbye, but its boundaries are fluid: the mother difficult to separate from her unborn child, dissolving without trace in the rivulets; the stanzas themselves running together, linked one to the other by rhyme (them/stem) or assonance (glints/wince).

If we look at stanzas six to eight, we can see how carefully Plath has patterned the poem. The foetus has relaxed its 'doll grip' but Plath makes that a matter for self-reproach, as I read it. Whereas even a cloud has a shadow attached, she has lost hers, is 'less constant' in an implicit comparison with the 'faithful' cypresses, rooted in the ground and thus in accumulated leaf mould, 'their heaped losses', able to draw life out of death. (Why does she say 'I am too happy'? Too happy for what? Does the sentence disturb the tenor of the poem?) The speaker, dazzled by sun on water, has briefly undertaken her own 'blind journey'; now the foetus does the same, too undeveloped for sight, and the water among the winter grass travels to its unknown end also. How subtle the alliteration is here: 'spindling rivulets / Unspool and spend themselves' – the domestic and the natural combine in a sense of inevitable yet constricted movement; again in 'thin as a skin seaming a star' the alliteration is unobtrusive yet binding, taking up the image of a fragile kind of healing.

The general journey into oblivion is halted, finally, by an evocation of 'your sister's birthday picture' – not the living daughter herself, just a bright, almost breathing picture. Despite the 'orange pompoms', its tones are predominantly blue. The 'indigo nimbus' scarcely sounds comforting – this may be a retrospective judgement on my part, remembering the lines 'I hear an owl cry / From its cold indigo' ('Event', p. 194) – and the 'little pale blue hill' is only a slightly softened version of the 'bald hill' of the opening. After this coolness comes the 'old dregs, the old difficulties' of marriage. Presumably it was the picture and the simple action of entering the 'lit house' that Plath was referring to when she described the speaker's world as 'vital and demanding'. Her description seems much more positive than the ending of the poem appears to me – what do you think?

Women's poetry this century has generally been much more open about the body and all its functions than men's: readiness to display mental distress has been matched by a willingness to reveal the body as it changes, ages, and is damaged. Some feminist criticism, especially in French, has been concerned with the female body as the site of pleasure, and has linked the celebration of physicality, carnality – not in the idealized form traditional to male writers – with the act of writing: they argue that the kind of language women use, and their syntax – often perceived by men as irrational and incoherent – embodies the fluid contours of their sexuality, unconfined in a way that man's phallic, linear sexual experience is not. In celebrating their own bodies, women move towards self-acceptance (the first readers of Anne Sexton's poetry, for example, were disconcerted by her frankness about menstruation). Other feminist critics have pointed out how deeply much women's poetry identifies the body with pain and repression, thus continuing the nineteenth-century association of feminine sensibility with suffering. Women writing in this tradition, at the mercy of their physical vulnerability, are impelled to self-rejection. Plath's work falls plainly within the latter tradition: while 'Parliament Hill Fields' has a disembodied speaker, other poems are physically extremely explicit: 'Grievously purpled, mouth skewered on a groan' ('The Ravaged Face'); 'I am lungless / And ugly, my belly a silk stocking / Where the heads and tails of my sisters decompose' ('Zoo Keeper's Wife'); 'Old sock-face, sagged on a darning egg' ('Face Lift', p. 155); the whole of 'The Surgeon at 2 a.m.' – you can add your own examples. Such explicitness is countered in Plath's work both by the image of body as stone, and by a desire to transcend the body altogether, shaking off mortality. The last stanza of 'Love Letter' (p. 147) offers a poignant paradigm of the whole process:

> I started to bud like a March twig:
> An arm and a leg, an arm, a leg.
> From stone to cloud, so I ascended.
> Now I resemble a sort of god
> Floating through the air in my soul-shift
> Pure as a pane of ice. It's a gift.

Does this rejection of the self as flesh extend to the self as mind? If the soul floats free of the body, transparent, can the mind also become less opaque, allowing the unconscious to surface? The French feminist philosopher, Julia Kristeva, maintains that many women can let

> what she calls the 'spasmodic force' of the unconscious disrupt their language because of their strong links with the pre-Oedipal mother-figure. But if these unconscious pulsations were to take over the subject entirely, the subject would fall back into pre-Oedipal or imaginary chaos and develop some form of mental illness.... the symbolic order is a patriarchal order, ruled by the Law of the Father, and any subject who tries to disrupt it, who lets unconscious forces slip through the symbolic repression, puts her or himself in a position of revolt against this regime.[6]

Sylvia Plath's work fits into this schema almost too neatly – 'Ariel' and 'Lady Lazarus', which we will shortly consider, are good examples. Several critics, notably David Holbrook,[7] have read Plath's poetry as the sick product of a sick mind. But Plath is able to take her own pulse, as Helen Vendler points out in an illuminating comparison of Plath with Anne Sexton and Emily Dickinson. Dickinson has no truck with the idea of insanity as 'normative': her poems provide a religious, philosophical and cosmic contrast against which the self is measured, and the drop into madness also.[8]

> I felt a Funeral, in my Brain,
> And Mourners to and fro
> Kept treading – treading – till it seemed
> That Sense was breaking through –

And when they all were seated,
A Service, like a Drum –
Kept beating – beating – till I thought
My Mind was going numb –

And then I heard them lift a Box
And creak across my Soul
With those same Boots of Lead, again,
Then Space – began to toll,

As all the Heavens were a Bell,
And Being, but an Ear,
And I, and Silence, some strange Race
Wrecked, solitary, here –

And then a Plank in Reason, broke,
And I dropped down, and down –
And hit a World, at every plunge,
And Finished knowing – then –[9]

You can see from this poem – unusually long for Dickinson – how Kristeva's remarks might apply to her, too: curiously enough, Dickinson replied to her first baffled reader, 'You think my gait "spasmodic." I am in danger, Sir.'[10] Her poems have the immediacy that seems, a century later, to authenticate an individual genius; their provisonal, unfinished quality is a rebellion against accepted poetic form, and even when conducted in the confined, reclusive environment of Dickinson's home in Amherst, Massachusetts, it courted the danger of disequilibrium – 'I felt a Cleaving in my Mind – / As if my Brain had split . . .'.[11]

So if this kind of experience had been voiced half a century before confessional poetry, what did Plath mean by saying that Lowell's breakthrough in *Life Studies* had been into areas 'partly taboo'? It is true that the originality of Dickinson's poetry was not appreciated in her lifetime: her first collection was published posthumously in 1890, but the rhymes and metre had been smoothed out, the metaphors made more 'sensible'; it was not until 1955 that a full, unvarnished text became available. And going further back, John Clare, a successful poet in the 1820s, spent his last twenty-four years in Northampton Asylum, still writing and indeed conscious that his private world of madness bore some relation to a reality existing outside it; much of his best work has only been published in the last fifty years.[12] Thus it could be said that while poets have not shied away from the subject of mental illness, editors and critics have been slow to see the value of their poems because of prevailing notions of what subjects, and forms, were properly poetic. For Plath, who was so concerned with what was acceptable, the establishment by

Lowell and others of what was, in effect, a new convention, was liberating.

In the 1960s, influenced by new psychoanalytical work such as R.D. Laing's *The Divided Self*, certain critics were reluctant to use a word such as 'madness' which, they contended, was a matter of suppressive establishment labelling: mental illness was not an appropriate category, it was a case of differing – often superior – visions of the world. This was perhaps a necessary corrective to the easy dismissal, both clinical and social, of people who did not conform to society's norms and were conveniently labelled and put away. But it also led, in literary circles at least, to a kind of privileging of mental illness as a guarantee of genius. On the one hand this destruction of taboos was a release for poets:

> Nearly all his adult life [Roethke] was a manic-depressive, subject to intermittent crack-ups of devastating violence. In the beginning he was terribly ashamed of these episodes and tried to conceal them ... The onset of his best work coincided with his discovery that he need not feel guilty about his illness; that it was a condition he could explore and use; that it was, in fact, convertible into daemonic energy, the driving power of imagination.[13]

On the other, it could lead to self-indulgence: the alliance of genius with madness has a long history, but to suffer the one does not mean to possess the other. Robert Lowell, writing to Roethke in 1963, said that their generation was marked out by a 'strange fact':

> It's this, that to write we seem to have to go at it with such single-minded intensity that we are always on the point of drowning ... I feel it's something almost unavoidable, some flaw in the motor. There must be some kind of glory to it all that people coming later will wonder at.[14]

Plath did not have the comfort of belonging to a circle – like that of Roethke, Jarrell, Lowell, Berryman – whose members could monitor each other's poetic progress in the understanding of its psychic costs. Undeniable poetic intelligence can falter in these realms: do you think that 'Lady Lazarus', for example, crosses a poetic line from 'fierce subjectivity' to 'compulsive exhibitionism'?[15] Please read the poem now.

Plath is, in Sexton's terms, 'telling it true' here. At ten she had nearly drowned, at twenty she had tried to commit suicide, and a few months before writing the poem she had driven her car off the road, later confiding to Alvarez that it was a deliberately self-destructive act. **The poem has lost none of its power to shock: does that stem partly from such biographical knowledge, or is that** irrelevant? Plath certainly disclaimed the 'I' of the poem – or we could read her BBC introduction as a wishful self-portrait: 'the phoenix, the libertarian spirit, what you will. She is also just a good, plain, very resourceful woman' (p. 294). Does her comment do justice to the scope of the poem?

DISCUSSION

To begin with, the title might give us pause. There is something mocking in its alliteration, and something faintly damning, too. Dr Johnson's famous remark about a woman's preaching being like a dog's walking on its hind legs – 'It is not done well, but you are surprised to find it done at all' – has a similarly patronizing tone, present also in an expression such as 'lady doctor'; there is the implication that the attempt is amateur. Lazarus was raised from the dead by Christ; this woman, far from being an amateur, excels the man and raises herself – DIY resourcefulness indeed.

Does the immediately personal experience at the core of the poem become more 'objective', gain a wider application? How does Plath manipulate her 'experiences, even the most terrifying'? At first, surely, by the tone of black humour, set by the title and continued in the metaphor of suicide as strip-tease – a spectacle which reflects the voyeuristic nature of the audience as much as the exhibitionism (even desperation) of the performer. In this case the skin itself is peeled off: the conceit here seems Jacobean; the 'sticky pearls' later in the poem may remind us, too, of *The Tempest*, skewing Ariel's image of the beautiful body changed in death by drowning. But more disturbing than this reclothed cadaver is the early comparison 'my skin / Bright as a Nazi lampshade'. There was a Nazi commandant whose wife had lampshades made of human skin: what purpose does the allusion serve here? Is it deliberately offensive to our sensibilities?

The speaker pits her voice against the traditional bearers of power, given an explicitly Nazi gloss by the prefix 'Herr': doctor, enemy, God, Lucifer. The doctor is always a potent type of male dominance (see also *Three Women*), but especially in Plath's experience of illness; moreover, the image of the Nazi doctors experimenting in the concentration camps has a peculiar horror. The references to religion throughout the poem are mocking, even blasphemous, as in 'These are my hands / My knees', alluding to the broken body of Christ on the cross – experimented on, one might say, by his father. Apparently the speaker can dispense with them all. While they think she is their own work, and can be destroyed at their will, her will exceeds their conception of her –

as pitiful victim, like those incinerated in the Nazi camps – and she rises like a phoenix from the ashes of their desired ending.[16] As in 'Daddy', I think, Plath's use of the fate of the Jews as metaphor is profoundly, not merely superficially, shocking. Shocking because it uses genocide as a spotlight to illuminate the speaker's own condition, appropriates it for egotistical purposes. The exhibitionism is deliberate: and then the poet taunts the reader for being a voyeur.

The impact of the poem's imagery is inseparable from the force of its language and rhythms – extraordinarily varied and brilliantly controlled. Plath described the poem as 'light verse': can you see why? It is a virtuoso performance, what Helen Vendler aptly calls 'a tantrum of style'.[17] 'Tantrum' directs us to that element in the poem – in Plath? – of almost childish defiance, the 'I'll show them . . . what if I die, then they'd be sorry'. Does Plath indulge or criticize such an attitude in 'Lady Lazarus'? Many readers have found Plath's brusque, taunting, slangy tone in this and other poems liberating in its effect. Why? Because they feel that at last an anger has come to the surface that had been boiling in women's lives for centuries, an anger caused by relentless masculine exploitation – this is where they locate the wider, impersonal resonance of the poem. Plath asked herself in her journals what was to be done with anger. Directed inward, it was corrosive of any identity painfully constructed; directed outward, it provided a negative kind of identity, as long as the performance was admired and applauded.

When Lowell was asked once why he was so much praised and esteemed, he replied: 'It may be that some people have turned to my poems because of the very things that are wrong with me. I mean the difficulty I have with ordinary living . . .'.[18] Plath, unlike Lowell, was perfectly competent about practical matters, indeed prided herself on that. Nevertheless, is it the difficulties she has with living that provide some of her fascination? Is she in fact able to make 'a poetic ritual of mourning for the previously unnameable or unspeakable'?[19]

Plath used ordinary events and everyday facts as a basis for larger, symbolic imaginings – the irrational and fantastic elements often arise from domestic situations. Her decision to keep bees, though, scarcely comes into the category of the ordinary. As we know, Otto Plath devoted much of his scholarly research to the ways of bumblebees; Plath had already described 'The Beekeeper's Daughter' (p. 118) in a poem dense with marriages and displacements, assigning the roles of king and queen. I assume that Plath's short story 'Among the Bumblebees' is directly autobiographical, centring on the power (and decline) of the godlike father who could subdue everything to his will:

> When it was the right time of year, her father took her into the garden and showed her how he could catch bumblebees. That was something no one else's father could do.... Alice liked to hear the angry, stifled buzzing of the bee, captured in the dark trap of her father's hand, but not stinging, not daring to sting. (*Johnny Panic*, p. 264)

Thus when she wrote her sequence of poems about beekeeping, larger issues of authority and passivity loom behind descriptions of ritual and season, which are in themselves extraordinarily vivid. I recommend that you read the sequence from 'The Bee Meeting' (p. 211) to 'Wintering' (p. 217), and although I shall concentrate here on the first poem, I should like you to keep the others in mind.[20] **What purpose do the repeated questions serve in these poems? What kind of self-discovery, if any, is going on in them? If she is able to inflate events, she also has enormous deflationary powers: do you see them at work here?**

DISCUSSION

Even in this short span, we can see a considerable change in style from 'The Beekeeper's Daughter' to 'The Bee Meeting', perhaps inseparable from a change in self-conception:

> Kneeling down
> I set my eye to a hole-mouth and meet an eye
> Round, green, disconsolate as a tear.

Puns are a way of closing the distance between things, momentarily confusing their separate identities; it is a device Plath likes to use. Here the eye/I is an inescapable pun – and what she sees becomes what she perceives herself to be: a green girl (no consort for the beekeeper), disconsolate. There has been a change in diction, too, since this poem was written in 1959 – how would you characterize it?

The opening of 'The Bee Meeting' reminds me of Auden's poems in the early 1930s: the same symbolic cast – 'the rector, the midwife, the sexton' – and setting, the apparently innocuous English village with its hidden menace; and the series of rhetorical questions. Here is Auden:

> The dog, the lady with the parcels, and the boy:
> There is the casual life outside the heart.

Yes, we are out of sight and earshot here.
Are you aware what weapon you are loading,
To what the talk is quietly leading?
Our pulses count but do not judge the hour.
Who are you with, from whom you turn away,
At whom do you dare not look? Do you know why?[21]

While Auden's speaking voice is studiedly neutral, dissociated from the events, Plath's is panic-stricken; despite her ostensible focus on event, the actual focus is the speaker.

The description of the speaker as 'nude as a chicken neck' effectively removes any dignity that might be associated with the ceremony of meeting. 'Nude' we associate with works of art, bodies that are sculptured, even magnificent; a chicken neck is peculiarly unlovely, somehow inert – and that underlying image of a corpse is reinforced by the way Plath describes the front opening of the borrowed smock as 'the slit from my neck to my knees', like a deathly gash temporarily repaired. Such a subset of images in the poem continues with the mention of blood-clots, anaesthetic, an operation, knives. What is the state of mind of someone who looks on this country landscape and sees illness and death?

Plath marks out the speaker for the community's attention. As in her poem 'Tulips' (p. 160), the impulse to be singular wars with the desire to belong. First of all she is too exposed, and the smock makes her blandly indistinguishable from her background; then her face is veiled (but beneath its 'fashionable white straw Italian hat', distinguishing the newcomer amidst the 'veils tacked to ancient hats'), so all is concealed. A real initiation perfectly symbolizes a larger rite of passage: behind this poem, the anxiety of the immigrant is discernible. How can she look as though she belongs?

The questions propel the poem along, but only from one state of ignorance to the next – this is not a poem of real discoveries. Why is the old queen bee so sought after? She is an ambivalent creature: hidden and procreative, authoritative yet powerless – and this is the 'self' Plath identifies with in 'Stings', 'red / Scar in the sky', whose flight is a wonderful escape but also a journey into death. The speaker's identification with both the queen bee and the sacrificial victim may suggest not an assumption of new roles but the old identities presented as a choice: woman as bitch goddess and woman as passive sufferer.

'The Bee Meeting' ends on questions: 'whose is that long white box?' suggests a coffin rather than any container of bees. Does the last stanza seem to develop from the rest of the poem – in the sense that it has all been concerned with a theatrical event (or an event made into theatre), although its backdrop is the essentially unthreatening world of an English village, with its rector and midwife, its beanflowers and hawthorn, its honey bees? Or does it seem to you a self-dramatization unrelated to the bee meeting, an abrupt change of persona? 'I am the magician's girl who does not flinch' sends us back to 'Lady Lazarus', with the readers as the peanut-crunching crowd who have paid to watch a ritual of incipient humiliation.

The next poem, 'The Arrival of the Bee Box', changes the perspective completely. The sinister box remains coffin-like, but it is 'only temporary'.

> I have simply ordered a box of maniacs.
> They can be sent back.
> They can die, I need feed them nothing. I am the owner.

Like Alice's father in the garden, she has authority over the bees: no longer a victim, 'Tomorrow I will be sweet God, I will set them free'.

Stan Smith makes the nice point that Plath's sense of the self is not at all fixed, or hierarchical, but

> *an ensemble of possibilities*, a 'swarm' of images, in which none takes precedence for more than a moment, and to which only a provisional coherence can be given. The self is both a rigid, false persona and an amorphous congeries, like the almost fluid bee-swarm, undergoing constant metamorphosis, continually dying and reborn in the mutations of the imagery.[22]

Please turn now to 'Ariel' (p. 239), written in the astonishingly fertile month of October 1962, and consider it in the light of Smith's description. **What are the metamorphoses that take place in the poem? Do the images coalesce, or develop, or remain separate? Do they connect with other poems by Plath?**

DISCUSSION

The poem is full of 'i' sounds, pushed into prominence at the ends and beginnings of lines so that it pulses with a sense of self, 'at one with the drive' of the syntax.

In *The Bell Jar*, Esther quotes her stuffy boyfriend's stuffier mother saying, 'What a man is is an arrow into the future and what a woman is is the place the arrow shoots off from' (p. 74), and when she is preparing to be seduced, thinks to herself, 'The last thing I wanted was infinite security and to be the place an arrow shoots off from. I wanted change and excitement and to shoot off in all directions myself, like the coloured arrows from a Fourth of July rocket' (p. 87). But the arrow in the poem is heading in one direction, toward the rising sun: a hopeful enough image, were it not that this arrow is also 'the dew that flies / Suicidal', evaporating as the heat increases.

The imagery is closely related to that of 'Stings'. Ariel, the *Oxford English Dictionary* notes, is the name given in the Old Testament to Jerusalem, and means 'Lion of god': here we have god's lionness, paralleling 'her lion-red body' in 'Stings'; the arrow flying into the sunrise (like the red comet); an escape from 'dead hands' like the escape from the mausoleum. But the violently swift movement from stasis to flight is not necessarily a deathly trajectory. Marjorie Perloff suggests that the dominant emotion of *Ariel* as a collection is not a death-wish but outrage and vengeful-ness.[23] In this context, it is possible to read 'Ariel' as a poem of sexual energy, whose climax is the 'little death' of the Jacobean poets, a consummation in which the creative and destructive energies are inseparable. There are strong sexual metaphors throughout, from the furrow to the berry to the red eye. (You will recognize the berry image from 'Blackberrying' – does it change here?)

Do the lines about the child's cry puzzle you, as they do me? One critic suggests that it is a murdered child – how would that fit the poem? If it is a poem about masturbation, as another critic has argued, then the lines could be interpreted as the failure to engender a child – the self-induced climax precluding any birth. Or if it is a poem that grows out of the release from domestic constraints, does it suggest the rider leaping a wall, further and further from the demands symbolized by a child's cry? Can it simultaneously hold these meanings?

The title returns us to *The Tempest*, not to a father-figure (as in 'Full Fathom Five') but to a spirit, an ethereal mischievous being who is the embodiment of poetry – 'the creative imaginative [projection]', as Plath had noted Auden's saying ten years pre-viously (*Journals*, p. 76). It was also the name of the horse on which Plath was learning to ride, on Dartmoor. The associations are those of release: Ariel like a genie from a bottle, eventually freed by his master Prospero to go his own way; the horse in motion an escape from domestic contraints at the least, even from thinking, an escape to pure physicality.

Do these poems about identity constitute a poetic autobiography in the sense that Lowell suggested when talking about *Life Studies*?

I've invented facts and changed things, and the whole balance of the poem was something invented. So there's a lot of artistry, I hope, in the poems. Yet there's this thing: if a poem is autobiographical... you want the reader to say, This is true... And so there was always that standard of truth which you wouldn't ordinarily have in poetry – the reader was to believe he was getting the real Robert Lowell.[24]

This implies a basic confidence that Plath simply did not have. But if she was less certain of her identity than Lowell, and much less concerned than he was to place herself in a recognizable historical context, her desire for artistry was as strong as his. Even when the subject is a loss of control, she endeavours to control its expression. Sometimes this emerges as coercion – as in the sustained but wilful metaphor of 'The Swarm'. At other times, the persona she chooses to embody her psychological dilemma is evidence of an egocentricity so powerful that it seals off rather than unsealing a world to our gaze. The element of self-absorption is real enough; the 'real Sylvia Plath' remains a matter for conjecture.

7. Speaking as a Woman

No matter how far or fast we travel, Plath declares in 'Totem',

There is no terminus, only suitcases

Out of which the same self unfolds like a suit
Bald and shiny, with pockets of wishes...

The unchanging self was an object both of loathing and of desire: the element of self-hatred is powerful in many of the poems we have looked at; there is also a recurrent longing for an unchanging self, not clothed in flesh but in stone, a self beyond the need or wish to alter.

Sustained poetic self-examination was not invented in the twentieth century: you may already have thought of Wordsworth's *Prelude* as an example. His poem, though, was subtitled 'or Growth of a Poet's Mind', and its form was dictated by his development as a poet, highlighting the moments or forces he perceived as having shaped his imagination. In this way Wordsworth could defend himself from charges of 'self-conceit': his poem concerned a vocation. Despite her strenuous training exercises for her art – the disciplines of note-taking, reading, keeping journals, and the arduous process of turning herself into a certain kind of prose writer – Plath's poetry does not present the self in the process of education, and rarely in the process of human change. More typical is the image of confrontation: old self with new self – each set in its mould – or self looking into a mirror and seeing, often, the threat to self, the possibility of extinction. Transformation is a magical thing, relying on an outside agency: sudden and complete, in effect it is a wish-fulfilment.

Let's look at 'Face Lift' (p. 155) and 'In Plaster' (p. 158) in these terms of confrontation and transformation. 'Some critics have invoked the word "schizophrenia" in talking about these poems, but Plath's sense of being several people at once never here goes beyond what everyone must at some time feel.'[1] Would you agree?

DISCUSSION

'Face Lift' is a fairytale in miniature. The transformation takes place under the aegis of an anaesthetist with froggy characteristics; he will not turn into a prince, instead he allows the patient with the sagging face to turn into a smooth young woman. The very process is seductive: she is 'nude as Cleopatra'. The mother, associated with sickness ('holding a tin basin'), is made redundant: the speaker is 'Mother to myself'. In other poems the true self has been enclosed or hidden; here the old self is relegated to a specimen jar – so is the new self true or false? There is a suggestion that something vital has been lost in the transaction: 'He made me feel something precious / Is leaking from the fingervents'.[2] What is Plath's tone in 'Face Lift' – sympathetic, mocking, neutral?

Think back to 'The Stones' and its last line: 'I shall be good as new': these two later poems can be read as a variation on that persistent theme of mending. In 'Face Lift' the speaker achieves a literal rebirth, emerging 'Pink and smooth as a baby'. 'In Plaster' offers a more difficult recovery, but in its third stanza also has echoes of the earlier poem's ending:

The vase, reconstructed, houses
The elusive rose.

Ten fingers shape a bowl for shadows.
My mendings itch.

After the period of hibernation in 'The Stones' and 'Face Lift', the speakers are detached from their recent histories, but the mended body of 'In Plaster' has a symbiotic relationship with its swaddling, which takes on a life of its own. The reconstructed self cannot simply free itself of its past, or return to a prettier age. It has to battle for possession.

The idea of the double and the mirror-image, you will have noticed by now, is basic to Plath's way of thinking about herself. The division in her writing personality between the author of *Letters Home* – all the cake-baking, floor-painting, sewing children's nightgowns, splashing out on Jaeger clothes – and the author of, say, 'A Birthday Present' or 'The Applicant' is expressed straightforwardly in her *Journals*:

I cannot ignore this murderous self: it is there. I smell it and feel it, but I will not give it my name. . . . I have a good self, that loves skies, hills, ideas, tasty meals, bright colors. . . . I have this demon who wants me to run away screaming if I am going to be flawed, fallible. It wants me to think I'm so good I must be perfect. Or nothing. (1 October 1957, pp. 176–7)

The strength of 'In Plaster' lies in the delineation of the complex relation between two such selves.

At the beginning the differences between them are quite clear: the new person is pure, uncomplaining, patient and calm; the 'old yellow one' is restless, unattractive, violent. The relationship between them becomes something the speaker can manipulate, however, because she detects the need of the 'real saint' for love; at the same time, she cannot mend without the support of her less spectacular, accommodating double. Neither hatred nor condescension is an adequate response. Perhaps there can be a compromise between them, 'a kind of marriage'? That is rejected, too: 'I see it must be one or the other of us'. The ending seems ambiguous: will the speaker leave the plaster-cast behind as she travels to the country of health, or is the tone childishly defiant, the speaker determined on death to outwit her gaoler?[3]

The poem is an image of more than the relationship of sickness to health, though it is that – plaster-casts come in many, less

84 *Speaking as a Woman*

tangible forms. It is also a metaphor for questions of authority
and passivity. Plath must have been especially sensitive to the
notion that keeping quiet, looking pretty and being patient were
the acceptable modes of behaviour for wives and mothers: her
story 'Day of Success' (1960) suggests that women's magazines'
advice for holding on to husbands in a competitive world still had
some mileage. She could see the advantages of passivity, and it
tempted her. This is not simply a matter for women: it is nearly
always easier to accept a given situation than to assume responsibility for changing it.

You may have noticed that the poems written in the last two years
of Plath's life are less formally complex than her earlier work, and
computer-aided research has borne out this intuition. There are
many more sentences of over thirty-five words, for example, in
The Colossus than in *Winter Trees* (a volume of previously un-
collected poems from the period of *Ariel*), which correspondingly
has a large number of one- to five-word sentences. Similarly, an
indication of the richness of vocabulary measured by the number
of words used once – the usage that might be expected of someone
using a thesaurus – bears out the difference between her pre- and
post-1960 work.[4]

The difference, to some degree at least, lies in Plath's later
practice of reading poems out loud; the earlier poems, she found,
did not lend themselves to this at all. Undoubtedly the BBC work
she was getting was influential in encouraging her to think of the
speaking voice when writing. This was slightly before the mid-
1960s phenomenon of poetry readings, which are now an accepted
part of creating a poet's audience. Impersonality is made both
more difficult and easier by reading to an audience: the contact is
direct, the rhythm of the particular voice alters one's perception of
a poem, perhaps, and identifies the poet with the lyric 'I' of the
poem. But it is also a performance and allows for dramatization:
the actress assumes her part merely for the duration of the poem.
So Plath, reading 'Daddy', can 'be' the part-Jewish protagonist
with an Electra complex, and disclaim identification. That poem
perfectly fits Lowell's definition of the 'four musts for oral performance': 'humor, shock, narrative, and a hypnotic voice'.[5]

The poems we have been considering in this chapter are
notable examples of Plath's voice at its most controlled. There is
no sense that – to use her own image – the emotion is leaking out
between the lines, unable to be contained. Yet that is a sensation
other late poems give me, as though Plath were working through a

private experience which makes her 'terribly upset' but which is not available to us as readers. What she wants to say, and the means she allows herself to express it, are at odds with each other. Helen McNeil, in her excellent essay on Plath, has this to say about her use of the lyric poem: 'one function of the subjective lyric voice is to mask the acts of a deeper self while simultaneously tracing their presence by an otherwise inexplicable vehemence'.[6]

You might think back to 'Fever 103°' in the light of that comment, and contrast it with the tone of her very last poem, 'Edge' (p. 272) – please read the latter poem now. 'Edge' is as composed as the tomb effigy it describes, and yet it is only an *'illusion* of Greek necessity' (emphasis added). Is the 'necessity', dressed up in Greek clothing, a mask for an intensely subjective decision? If we think back to 'Electra on the Azalea Path' and Plath's own criticism of the poem as too forced and rhetorical, we can see that the later poem achieves the air of necessity that the earlier one too strenuously strives for: we are presented with a *fait accompli*.[7] **What do you make of the last two couplets of 'Edge', with their abrupt change of perspective? How do they relate to other lunar landscapes in Plath's poetry?**

DISCUSSION

Although I said earlier that Plath had a very positive attitude towards motherhood, reflected in the poems specifically about her children, there are asides in other poems that express resentment and impatience (in 'Stopped Dead', for instance). Here the children are pictured each as 'a white serpent' before they become as rose petals. They have drained the milk given by their mother, and thus, it would seem, contributed to her death by depleting her resources. Such a reading is reinforced by the discovery that serpents were the Greek symbol of Necessity: we have already considered the notion that the birth of a child carries the seed of the parents' death. This time, however, they all die together and the poem almost convinces us of the naturalness of this dead trio by moving from the stony, white images to the midnight garden where roses fold in their petals for the night – except that this too becomes deathly, the garden 'stiffens' like a corpse and 'odors bleed' from it.

The distance and indifference of this last poem disengages it from us, I think, in a way that most of her previous poems have not been disengaged from their readers. We may dislike earlier poems, or we might find them passionately persuasive accounts of certain emotional states, but this poem seems to exist independently, for itself: its surface is too smooth to allow us purchase. ('Contusion', written the previous day, is similar in its effects.) Having abandoned the 'I' voice in favour of describing 'the woman', and using blunt statement rather than dialogue with the reader (no questions are asked), Plath moves even further off in her lines about the moon. Its aloof attitude suggests what ours should be. But you may disagree, and interpret 'its blacks' as the garb of a mourner; the 'crackle and drag' as the sound of radio static, preventing the true message – this is only an illusion of necessity – from getting through.

At the beginning of her writing life, Plath had a very clear idea of her audience and the people she wanted to reach; she was prepared to tailor her work accordingly. It is clear that Ted Hughes's reading and criticism of her work was vital to its development, though perhaps inhibiting in some ways; when that working relationship ended with the break-up of their marriage, Plath felt that a great deal of repressed emotion was coming to the surface and increasingly she seemed to be writing for herself alone. Of course, she still wanted this work published, but, as we have seen in 'Lady Lazarus', she took a sardonic view of the 'peanut-crunching crowd' who would be paying to see the work of self-exposure. The risk-taking of the later work is the consequence of loosening deeply-entrenched self-controls, at uncontainable personal cost.

In some later poems – 'A Secret' or 'Eavesdropper', for example – rage and bitterness take over at the expense of the intelligence Plath required of poets. We can see why such poems would have been slow to find publishers, but this was also the case with more successful work. Plath's reputation has been a posthumous affair, necessarily. The publication of *Ariel* coincided with the rise of the women's movement in America, and gave her life a paradigmatic quality especially susceptible to feminist interpretation: the bright woman caught between her ambitions as an artist and her expectations as a middle-class female; the psychoanalytical treatment that was abandoned before it could address this conflict in terms of a larger problem about patriarchal authority; the terms and failure of her marriage; her poetry which was stigmatized, even by sympathetic male critics, with the adjectives 'shrill' and 'hysterical'.

Stan Smith, in his sophisticated essay on Plath's poetry and the concept of history, has suggested that she has a particular understanding of the way 'the self is constructed as a *subject*, a being not only aware of itself but *subjected to* the authority of the

family and state': one of the key moments in the process of
construction is the period in which sexual identity is acquired.

> This is why Plath's poetry has been so powerfully and appropriately
> co-opted by the Women's Movement.... Painfully aware of the
> competing male and female inflexions in her personality, Plath con-
> tinually returns to this 'mirror phase' in the child's early evolution –
> the point at which it perceives, in the mirror of the mother's eyes,
> and then in its own internalised mirror, the sexually specific identity
> it is expected to assume. Before this point, all is decentred and
> dispersed, a welter of images and options without a cohering focus.
> When Plath's poetry returns to the image of the mirror it returns too
> to the frontier of a realm where images spawn and proliferate and
> the unitary ego dissolves...[8]

Obviously the appeal of Plath's work is not confined to women,
because the extremes of emotion in which she deals, on that 'edge'
where familiar boundaries and constructed certainties fray and
give way, are not the prerogative of one gender. Nevertheless, her
dilemmas – especially her feelings of anger and effacement – have
been most persistently explored by women over the last two
decades. I have drawn on some feminist criticism in writing this
book: Plath's poetry encourages 'martyrology', but her critics have
become more subtle over the last twenty years. Ostriker is a good
example, her work both sympathetic and discriminating. Sandra
M. Gilbert subtitled her influential essay on Plath, 'Confessions of
a Plath Addict': 'All of us who read her traced our own journey in
hers ... from college to villanelles to babies to the scary skeletons
of poems we began to study, now, as if they were sacred writ.'[9]
This element of identification has remained: from time to time
there are still angry exchanges of letters in the British press over
Plath's gravestone, which is inscribed 'Sylvia Plath Hughes', an
inscription seen as a wrongful incorporation of 'Sylvia Plath' into
the patriarchy that had a hand in her destruction. Women have
felt that if only she had been able to hang on – with the help of
good female friends – she might have discovered an identity she
could live with as the women's movement gained strength in the
decade after her death. Few poets of this century have aroused
such proprietarial feeling: it makes criticism difficult, and biography a minefield.

While this poetry speaks directly to many women, they have
to acknowledge the hostility towards women present in it. Barbara
Hardy makes a persuasive case for *Three Women* as a politicized
attack on man and his powers ('They are so jealous of everything
that is not flat!'), but also remarks that at almost every point
in Plath's poetry the feminine tradition stands for the negative

qualities of the consumer society: its possessiveness, materialism, competitiveness, hypocrisy.[10] The 'disquieting muses' of the early poems hover in the background, and emerge in *Three Women* inextricably linked with the forces wrecking the planet:

> The trees wither in the street. The rain is corrosive.
> I taste it on my tongue, and the workable horrors,
> The horrors that stand and idle, the slighted godmothers
> With their hearts that tick and tick, with their satchels of
>   instruments.

You may wish to use these lines – and others – to defend Plath against the charge so often made against her, implicitly and explicitly, of narrowly egotistic subject matter. Critics have certainly interpreted her poetry not only in a wider context of women's experience, but also of concern with the larger issues of power and passivity that corrupt relations between State or Church and people. In this regard, you may like to analyse 'The Applicant' (p. 221), or 'The Swarm' (p. 215). You may want to look back to the discussion of the natural world, which I argued was rarely described for its own sake, in the light of the peculiarly poised poems 'Among the Narcissi' and 'Pheasant', which say something about illness and death in ways quite divorced from Plath's own predicament.

What should we expect, though, of a poet who died so young? She had been through experiences that were not untypical of her sex: university, marriage, children, a husband's infidelity, being a single parent – even the early death of her father and her suicide attempts were not extraordinary. She did not have the different perspective on these events that more years – and, who knows, more sophisticated medication – would have allowed. Writing in her journal in January 1959, Plath records reading the poems of Adrienne Rich – perhaps *The Diamond Cutters* (1955) – 'they stimulate me: they are easy yet professional, full of infelicities and numb gesturings at something, but instinct with "philosophy", what I need' (p. 293). Rich was thirty at the time, and working on her third collection, *Snapshots of a Daughter-in-Law*, which was published the year Plath died. She later described writing the title poem as 'an extraordinary relief', the beginning of a new kind of writing out of her experience as a woman, and as a politically conscious woman. If you have not read any of Rich's poetry, let me recommend it to you: a very rare example of a woman's public voice that does not sacrifice any of its private resonance. I am not saying that events in the 1960s would have opened up Plath's poetry in this direction, but simply that her voice has been cut off in its thirty-first year, restricted to certain tones. Think of Yeats, who was still writing poems in the style of 'The Song of Wandering Aengus' in his late twenties, and was not to renounce his earlier style until he was forty-seven, throwing away the song which was 'a coat / Covered with embroideries / Out of old mythologies' for the greater enterprise of 'walking naked'.

It is clear that Plath knew she was writing a new kind of poetry in the 1960s, as her remarks about the change to a speaking voice indicate. Did she, therefore, conceive of poetry itself differently? How does she write about the act of writing? Two poems and two lines come to mind in this context: 'Poems, Potatoes' (p. 106) and 'Words' (p. 270) – what have they in common? Entirely different in construction, the earlier one sticking to its chosen metaphors, the later constantly dissolving and replacing them, they both express dissatisfaction and eventually despair with the medium of language itself.[11] The following two lines are from 'Kindness': 'The blood jet is poetry; / There is no stopping it.' We have already noted that Plath connected writing with health, but this is an even more intimate relationship, and Plath made the body–poetry connection, too, when she wrote about the poets that gave her most pleasure as being 'possessed by their poems as by the rhythms of their own breathing. Their finest poems seem born all-of-a-piece, not put together by hand...'.[12] While writing a poem she could feel magnificent, but afterwards the feeling could not be sustained. If poetry is lifeblood, despairing of poetry is also to despair of life.

Thoreau defined poetry as 'a piece of very private history, which inostentatiously lets us into the secret of a man's life'. Much poetry of the later twentieth century has simply dropped that effort in favour of ostentation. We return to the vexed question of how the secret of a life is presented: Yeats said he was 'walking naked', but surely he was constructing a new mythology out of the momentous period of Irish history he inhabited? And according to Hughes, Plath was writing not occasional poems but one long poem,

> chapters in a mythology where the plot, seen as a whole and in retrospect, is strong and clear – even if the origins of it and the *dramatis personae* are at bottom enigmatic. The world of her poetry is one of emblematic visionary events, mathematical symmetries, clairvoyance and metamorphoses.[13]

Indeed, as we have found, situations, images, colours, occur again and again, creating a web of associations. The lunar image is a good example: if in classical mythologies the moon has been a symbol of both chastity and fertility – and Plath would have found all this spelt out in Robert Graves's book *The White Goddess*, by which Hughes was deeply influenced – then Plath chose to emphasize its negative associations: sterility, flatness, indifference. Its relation to the menstrual cycle is similarly a matter of discouraging repetition, dragging the female tides in its wake. Hughes takes the line that nothing but the poems of *Ariel* justifies our interest in Plath, or our reading of her other work: everything was a route to that collection. Would you agree?

Stephen Spender has suggested that even Plath's best poems 'have little principle of beginning or ending, but seem fragments, not so much of one long poem, as an outpouring which could not stop with the lapsing of the poet's hysteria'.[14] Feminist critics would want to read them in a different way: Sandra Gilbert suggests that they are deliberately imperfect because Plath had made the conscious decision that 'perfection is terrible', and that, rather than lacking control, they were the embodiment of Plath's desire that they should be possessed of the rhythms of breathing, be 'all of a piece' with the poet. Her poems raise the question of whether there is 'feminine writing' (*écriture feminine*), by its very nature difficult to read. 'Formlessness' has always been associated with women: it is based on their physiology, as Mary Ellmann points out, and when Joyce gives Molly Bloom her monologue in *Ulysses*, it is a liquid utterance. It is not, usually, a complimentary view of women's minds. The French critic Hélène Cixous has suggested that feminine writing (not a term she likes, and which she sees as independent of the sex of the writer – a woman may write in a masculine way and vice versa) is inseparable from the voice, it is an extension of speech. What is more, it is not simply her own voice but comes out of a deeper layer of the psyche, where the first voice is inscribed – the voice of the mother. Cixous also argues that the power of the writing woman's voice derives from the fact that she has erected few or no defence mechanisms against her earliest experiences, unlike the male who represses the mother's voice – and the generosity and openness that Cixous sees as characteristic of the mother.

The more pragmatic line of Anglo-Saxon feminist literary critics have found this perspective hard to adopt in their more political, less psycho-sexually orientated discourse. Nevertheless, it has a bearing on Plath's poetry, not only in the intimate linkage of the body with writing. Cixous sees such unguardedness as a positive strength; we can see it as a source both of power in Plath's writing and of vulnerability. If the lack of defence mechanisms left her more exposed to the voice of the mother – although Plath declared the first breathing she registered was that of the sea, the sea is in turn identified with the female element – and if her associations with that voice were not with what psychiatrists called 'the Good Mother' but with a demanding yet essentially submissive mother, then what did that mean for the poetic voice she struggled to find? Could she use this insecurity about her identity, entertain its contradictions, or do we find in the chains of imagery in *Ariel* those contradictions unresolved?

As critics have endeavoured to put her in the context of her age and of American culture, Plath appears less singular than in the decade after her death. Instead of romanticizing the suicidal tendencies of a generation, we can focus on its resilience, and on the level of linguistic energy achieved in its best poems. Plath's remain rare in their ability to reproduce for us mental and emotional states from which we flinch. Recognizing this still leaves us with what Hugh Kenner has called the 'hardest critical question' – certainly the hardest question from a humanist perspective:

> Given the fact that in a few poems Sylvia Plath illustrates an extreme state of existence, one at the very boundary of nonexistence, what illumination – moral, psychological, social – can be provided of either this state or the general human condition by a writer so deeply rooted in the extremity of her plight? Suicide is an eternal possibility of our life and therefore always interesting; but what is the relation between a sensibility so deeply captive to the idea of suicide and the claims and possibilities of human existence in general?[15]

You may reject the notion of humanism as outmoded, or of the whole business of suicide as in the end tangential to Plath's poetic achievement. All literary criticism can do is send you back to the poems, enabling you to read them differently, or more deeply, than you did at first, and clarifying your own response which springs from a time, place and education quite different from those of other critics, or indeed from the poet's.

> I think we ought to read only the kind of books that wound and stab us. If the book we're reading doesn't wake us up with a blow on the head, what are we reading it for? So that it will make us happy, you tell me? Good lord, we would be happy precisely if we had no books, and the kind of books that make us happy are the kind we could write ourselves, if we had to. But we need the books that affect us like a disaster, that grieve us deeply, like the death of someone we loved more than ourselves, like being banished into forests, far from everyone, like a suicide. A book must be the axe for the frozen sea inside us. That is my belief.[16]

Notes

Chapter 1 – Introduction: 'Over-exposed, like an X-ray'

1 Sylvia Plath, *Johnny Panic and the Bible of Dreams* (London: Faber & Faber, 1979).

2 Elizabeth Hardwick, *Seduction and Betrayal; women and literature* (New York: Vintage Books, 1975), p. 126.

3 Sylvia Plath, *Letters Home: correspondence 1950–1963*, ed. Aurelia Schober Plath (London: Faber & Faber, 1975).

4 Robert Lowell, 'Sylvia Plath's *Ariel*' in Lowell, *Collected Prose* (New York: Farrar, Straus & Giroux, 1987), p. 124. See also Mary Ellmann's remarks on this characterization of Plath in *Thinking About Women* (London: Virago, 1979), pp. 36–7.

5 Ted Hughes, *Poetry Book Society Bulletin* (Spring 1965).

6 Peter Orr (ed.), *The Poet Speaks* (London: Routledge & Kegan Paul, 1966), pp. 167–8.

7 Anne Sexton, 'The Barfly Ought to Sing' in Charles Newman (ed.), *The Art of Sylvia Plath* (London: Faber & Faber, 1970), p. 178.

8 Michael Kirkham, 'Sylvia Plath' in Linda M. Wagner (ed.), *Sylvia Plath: the critical heritage* (London: Routledge, 1988), p. 290.

9 M.L. Rosenthal, *The New Poets* (New York: Oxford University Press, 1967), p. 79.

10 Lowell, 'Sylvia Plath's *Ariel*', p. 122.

11 Ted Hughes's role as Plath's literary executor has been controversial. Reading with hindsight makes Plath's poems particularly liable to a one-directional interpretation. Marjorie Perloff has argued persuasively that this is partly the effect of Hughes's arrangement of *Ariel*, which in its published form is not shaped as Plath intended in November 1962. Her original contents list is provided at the end of the *Collected Poems*, and Hughes has noted that the collection began with the word 'Love' ('Morning Song') and ended with the word 'Spring' ('Wintering'). See Perloff, 'The Two *Ariels*: the (Re) Making of the Sylvia Plath Canon' in Neil Fraistat (ed.), *Poems in Their Place: the intertextuality and order of poetic collections* (Chapel Hill and London: University of North Carolina Press, 1986), pp. 308–33. There is also the matter of the *Journals*, which were published in North America in 1982 with a foreword by Hughes, but are not available in the United Kingdom. Like Leonard Woolf's early edition

of his wife's diaries, they have been edited with an eye to what is relevant to the writing, and to spare the feelings of living relatives and friends. It is unlikely, however, that they will ever be published in full as Woolf's have been, and Hughes admits to having destroyed a couple of the last notebooks immediately after Plath's death. Jacqueline Rose, in *The Haunting of Sylvia Plath* (London: Virago, 1991), has a detailed and eloquent discussion of the issue of ownership and control of Plath's work in her chapter 'The Archive'.

12 A. Alvarez, 'Sylvia Plath' (*The Review*, 9, October 1963), reprinted in Graham Martin and P.N. Furbank (eds), *Twentieth Century Poetry* (Milton Keynes: Open University Press, 1975), p. 439. Alvarez's view of Plath has been very influential in establishing a legendary poetic presence, particularly through his book about suicide and creativity, *The Savage God* (London: Weidenfeld & Nicolson, 1971).

Chapter 2 – 'What ceremony of words can patch the havoc?'

1 'Ode for Ted' (p. 29), for example, uses alliteration on the Anglo-Saxon poetic model, and the result is heavy-handed (the poem is also full of archaic usages); it is used to better effect, however, in 'Hardcastle Crags' (1957, p. 62).

2 Plath interviewed Wilbur for *Mademoiselle*. They met later, after her suicide attempt, when 'the published poet in his happiness' (as Wilbur ironically describes himself) was summoned to tea by a mutual friend in the hope of encouraging Plath to go on writing – indeed, living:

> How large is her refusal, and how slight
> The genteel chat whereby we recommend
> Life, of a summer afternoon, despite
> The brewing dusk which hints that it may end....
>
> ... Sylvia who, condemned to live,
> Shall study for a decade as she must,
> To state at last her brilliant negative
> In poems free and helpless and unjust.
>
> ('Cottage Street, 1953')

See Richard Wilbur, *Collected Poems* (London: Faber & Faber, 1990).

3 Ted Hughes and Frances McCullough (eds), *The Journals of Sylvia Plath*, (New York: Ballantine Books edition, 1983).

4 If a directly psychological reading of the poem interests you, see Anne Stevenson's interpretation in her biography of Plath, *Bitter Fame* (London: Viking, 1989), pp. 125–7.

5 Hughes notes in the *Collected Poems* that 'The Moon and the Yew Tree', written as late as 1961, was one of the assignments he gave her.

6 Interview in *Mademoiselle*, January 1959. Quoted by Edward Butscher, *Sylvia Plath: Method and Madness* (New York: The Seabury Press, 1976), p. 233.

7 This remark was made in the course of a reading in Massachusetts, recorded for the Library of Congress (April 1958), quoted by Butscher, *Sylvia Plath*, pp. 228–9.

8 Eric Homberger, *The Art of the Real* (London: Dent, 1977), p. 108.

Curiously enough Roethke's father, like Plath's, was called Otto and was a Germanic disciplinarian; his greenhouses were a source of imagery to Roethke in the way that Otto Plath's work with bees was to his daughter. Section II of Roethke's five-part poem 'The Lost Son' has clear affinities with 'Poem for a Birthday':

> Where do the roots go?
> Look down under the leaves.
> Who put the moss there?
> These stones have been here too long.
> Who stunned the dirt into noise?
> Ask the mole, he knows.
> I feel the slime of a wet nest.
> Beware Mother Mildew.
> Nibble again, fish nerves.

('The Pit')

See Theodore Roethke, *Selected Poems* (London: Faber & Faber, 1969), p. 17.
9 Hughes, *PBS Bulletin*.

Chapter 3 – Poet and Mother

1 Adrienne Rich, 'When We Dead Awaken' in Rich, *On Lies, Secrets and Silence* (London: Virago, 1980), p. 42.
2 Sandra M. Gilbert, 'A Fine, White Flying Myth: the Life/Work of Sylvia Plath' in Sandra M. Gilbert and Susan Gubar (eds), *Shakespeare's Sisters: feminist essays on women poets* (Bloomington: Indiana University Press, 1979), p. 255.
3 Donald Hall, 'My Son, My Executioner' in Hall, *The One Day and Poems 1947–1990* (Manchester: Carcanet Press, 1991) p. 19.
4 Rich, 'When We Dead Awaken', pp. 40–1.
5 Alice Suskin Ostriker, *Stealing the Language: the emergence of women's poetry in America* (London: The Women's Press, 1987), p. 62.
6 Wimsatt, quoted in Catherine Belsey, *Critical Practice* (London: Methuen, 1980), p. 15. This is a good general introduction to critical theory.
7 If you would like to compare it with a poem that answers such expectations with a thoughtful grace, read Eavan Boland's 'Night Feed' in her *Selected Poems* (Manchester: Carcanet Press; Dublin: WEB, 1989).
8 There is a good, extended analysis of 'Nick and the Candlestick' in Barbara Hardy's essay 'The Poetry of Sylvia Plath', in Hardy, *The Advantage of Lyric* (London: Athlone Press, 1977), pp. 122–7.
9 Hughes, *PBS Bulletin*.

Chapter 4 – Poet as Daughter, or Father as Muse?

1 George Steiner suggests that Plath took this image from *The Duchess of Malfi*: 'When I look into the fish-pond in my garden, / Methinks I

see a thing armed with a rake'; see 'Dying is an Art' in Steiner, *Language and Silence* (New York: Atheneum, 1976), p. 296.

2 Virginia Woolf died by drowning, putting large stones in her pockets. Plath frequently refers to Woolf's writing in the journal; 'But her suicide, I felt I was reduplicating in that black summer of 1953. Only I couldn't drown' (*Journals*, p. 152).

3 Eliot's sources were Jessie L. Weston's book on the Grail legend, *From Ritual to Romance*, and James Frazer's *The Golden Bough*, which has been an immensely influential work.

4 Rich, 'When We Dead Awaken', p. 35.

5 Ostriker, *Stealing the Language*, p. 236.

6 The later poem 'Medusa' (p. 224), which we might instinctively associate with myth, in fact takes its title from the generic term for jellyfish – of which a type is *Aurelia aulita* (moon jellyfish). Its bitter, jangling dismissiveness makes 'The Disquieting Muses', her other poem about the mother figure, look positively sedate.

7 James Thrall Soby, *Giorgio de Chirico* (New York: Museum of Modern Art, 1955), p. 25.

8 This is the line taken by Susan Bassnett in *Sylvia Plath* (London: Macmillan, 1987): she maintains that the speaker is a woman who knows her place, duty and history but is far from being crushed by that knowledge.

9 Plath had read the Grimms' fairytales among others, but she had also read commentaries, and in 1958 had noted the work of Oesterreich on *Possession: Demoniacal and Other*: 'These visions of demons are the objective figures of angers, remorse, panic' (*Journals*, p. 256). How much is the demon father an image of Plath's own destructive impulses? Helen Vendler points out that 'Fairy tales and folk tales put forth a child's black-and-white ethics', and suggests that was why they appealed to Anne Sexton's 'childlike and vengeful mind'; see *The Music of What Happens* (Cambridge, Massachusetts and London: Harvard University Press, 1988), p. 303. Might this also apply to Plath?

10 Vendler, *The Music of What Happens*, p. 281.

11 Quoted by Klaus Wagenbach, *Franz Kafka: pictures of a life* (New York: Pantheon Books, 1984), p. 186.

12 Steven Gould Axelrod points out that Otto Rank in *Beyond Psychology* (a book Plath read and underlined for her undergraduate thesis) explicitly compares women to Jews, since 'woman . . . has suffered from the very beginning a fate similar to that of the Jew, namely suppression, slavery, confinement, and subsequent persecution'. Rank also 'argues that Jews speak a language of pessimistic "self-hatred" that differs essentially from the language of the majority cultures in which they find themselves', and suggests analogies with women's use of language. See Axelrod, *Sylvia Plath: the wound and the cure of words* (Baltimore and London: Johns Hopkins University Press, 1990), p. 55.

13 Peter Orr (ed.), *The Poet Speaks*, p. 169.

14 A. Alvarez, *The New Poetry* (Harmondsworth: Penguin, revised edition 1966), p. 25.

15 Quoted by Dennis Walder, *Ted Hughes* (Milton Keynes: Open
   University Press, 1987), p. 31.
16 Theodor W. Adorno, *Prisms* (Cambridge, Massachusetts: MIT Press,
   1981), p. 34.
17 The poem begins 'I do not know why / I should be so sad . . .'. It was
   so well known that the Nazis could not erase it from anthologies, but
   as Heine was Jewish, all reference to him was suppressed and it was
   credited to 'Anon'.
18 You might like to read a poem by Randall Jarrell, the troubled
   American poet who died in uncertain circumstances soon after Plath,
   'Deutsch Durch Freud', which opens: 'I believe my favorite country's
   German'. This was a purely linguistic choice for him.
19 Steiner, *Language and Silence*, p. 301.
20 Seamus Heaney, 'The Indefatigable Hoof-taps: Sylvia Plath' in
   Heaney, *The Government of the Tongue* (London: Faber & Faber,
   1988), p. 165.

Chapter 5 – 'Is there no way out of the mind?'

1 Peter Orr (ed.), *The Poet Speaks*, p. 167.
2 Samuel Taylor Coleridge, *Notebooks*, ed. Kathleen Coburn, vol. 2
  1804–1808 (text) (London: Routledge & Kegan Paul, 1962), extract
  2546.
3 Ted Hughes, *Poetry in the Making* (London: Faber & Faber, 1967),
  p. 76.
4 W.H. Auden, 'American Poetry', reprinted in *The Dyer's Hand*
  (London: Faber & Faber, 1975), pp. 358, 364.
5 Elizabeth Hardwick, *Seduction and Betrayal*, pp. 127–8.
6 A propos of this poem, Hughes remarked: 'It's my suspicion that no
  poem can be a poem that is not a statement from the powers in
  control of our life, the ultimate suffering and decision in us. It seems
  to me that this is poetry's only real distinction from the literary forms
  we call "not poetry".' See 'Notes on the Chronological Order of
  Sylvia Plath's Poems', in Charles Newman (ed.), *The Art of Sylvia
  Plath*, p. 194.
7 Peter Orr, *The Poet Speaks*, p. 171. Plath declared herself interested
  in novels because of the sort of detail they could accomodate: 'I feel
  that in a novel, for example, you can get in toothbrushes and all the
  paraphernalia that one finds in daily life, and I find this more difficult
  in poetry. . . . I'm a woman, I like my little *Lares* and *Penates*, I like
  trivia . . .'. In an interview in 1961, Robert Lowell suggested that
  contemporary poetry had become too much of a craft: '. . . perhaps
  there has never been such skill. Yet the writing seems divorced from
  the culture. It's become too much something specialized that can't
  handle much experience. . . . Prose is in many ways better off than
  poetry.' (*Collected Prose*, p. 244). Perhaps what Plath was discarding
  as peripheral to poetry was in fact the dailiness of experience that
  helps to preserve sanity.
8 She had used the line before, '. . . the grasses / Unload their griefs on
  my shoes', in 'Private Ground' (p. 130).

9 Compare this number with 166 references to white, 158 to black; 78 to light, 72 to dark. See Richard M. Matovich, *A Concordance to the Collected Poems of Sylvia Plath* (New York and London: Garland, 1986).

10 See Michael Kirkham's discussion of the poem in Linda W. Wagner (ed.), *Sylvia Plath: the critical heritage*, pp. 281–3.

11 Seamus Heaney discusses the draft and 'Elm' in *The Government of the Tongue*, pp. 160–62.

12 Robert Pinsky, *The Situation of Poetry* (Princeton, NJ: Princeton University Press, 1976), p. 119.

13 Ibid., p. 130.

14 Ortner's essay is reprinted in Michelle Zimbalist Rosaldo and Louise Lamphere (eds), *Women, Culture and Society* (Stanford, CA: Stanford University Press, 1974). Nancy Chodorow's essay in the same volume, 'Family Structure and Feminine Personality', offers some insights into feminine personality development that bear interestingly on Plath's situation and poetry. For Ostriker's commentary, see her *Stealing the Language*, pp. 114–15.

15 Vendler, *The Music of What Happens*, p. 276.

Chapter 6 – Self-Portraits

1 A. Alvarez, 'A Talk with Robert Lowell', *Encounter*, 24 (February 1965), p. 43.

2 Lowell, *Collected Prose*, p. 103 (emphasis added); see also Ostriker, *Stealing the Language*, pp. 3–4.

3 Adrienne Rich, 'When We Dead Awaken', p. 39. Plath sent Moore a batch of her early poems, and was distressed by her response: 'don't be so grisly', 'you are too unrelenting' (*Journals*, p. 250). She later noted that she was 'reading Elizabeth Bishop with great admiration. Her fine originality, always surprising, never rigid, flowing, juicier than Marianne Moore, who is her godmother' (*Journals*, p. 319).

4 Peter Orr (ed.), *The Poet Speaks*, p. 169.

5 'Mourning and Melancholia' (1917), *The Standard Edition of the Complete Works of Sigmund Freud*, trans. and ed. James Strachey (London: The Hogarth Press, 1957), vol. XIV, pp. 245–7.

6 Toril Moi, *Sexual / Textual Politics: feminist literary theory* (London: Routledge, 1985), pp. 11–12.

7 David Holbrook, *Sylvia Plath: poetry and existence* (London: Athlone Press, 1976).

8 Vendler, *The Music of What Happens*, p. 308.

9 Thomas H. Johnson (ed.), *The Complete Poems of Emily Dickinson* (London: Faber & Faber 1970; 1975), Poem 280.

10 Ibid., p. vii. Lyndall Gordon has suggested that we see Plath's 'introspectiveness, her strenuousness, her horror and macabre humour' in the New England tradition of Dickinson and Eliot: *Poetry Review* 79:4 (Winter 1989–90), p. 60.

11 *The Complete Poems of Emily Dickinson*, Poem 937.

12 Robert Pinsky compares Plath's 'Poppies in July' not only with Roethke but also with John Clare's poem 'Badger' in his suggestive

section on 'Wonder and Derangement' in *The Situation of Poetry*.

13 'Stanley Kunitz: an interview' in Robert Boyers (ed.), *Contemporary Poetry in America – essays and interviews* (New York: Schocken Books, 1974), p. 38.

14 Quoted by Marjorie Perloff, '*Poètes Maudits* of the Genteel Tradition', in Steven Gould Axelrod and Helen Deese (eds), *Robert Lowell: essays in the poetry* (Cambridge: Cambridge University Press, 1986), p. 106.

15 Stanley Kunitz, when asked whether he felt kinship with the confessional school, replied (in part): 'I've always admired a fierce subjectivity; but compulsive exhibitionism – and there's plenty of that around – gobs of sticky hysteria – are an embarrassment. . . . you can say anything as long as it's true – But not everything that's true is worth saying' (Boyers, *Contemporary Poetry*, p. 38).

16 Seamus Heaney thinks that the use she makes of myth in this poem is too particularized: '. . . the cultural resonance of the original story is harnessed to a vehemently self-justifying purpose, so that the supra-personal dimensions of knowledge – to which myth typically gives access – are slighted in favour of the intense personal need of the poet' (*The Government of the Tongue*, p. 168).

17 Vendler, *The Music of What Happens*, p. 282. She provides an excellent analysis of Plath's language and tone in 'Lady Lazarus'.

18 Lowell to Stanley Kunitz, quoted by Ian Hamilton in *Robert Lowell: a biography* (London: Faber & Faber, 1983), p. 309.

19 I am indebted for this formulation to Nicole Jordan.

20 You may also want to compare the notes on the bee meeting reprinted in *Johnny Panic* (pp. 240–44) with the poem about the same event. The prose version is altogether more gossipy and particularized. Half mocking herself, Plath mentions that she called upon her father's protection from bee-stings.

21 Poem 9, *The English Auden: poems, essays and dramatic writings 1927–1939*, ed. Edward Mendelson (London: Faber & Faber, 1977), p. 149.

22 Stan Smith, 'Waist-Deep in History: Sylvia Plath' in Smith, *Inviolable Voice: history and twentieth-century Poetry* (Atlantic Highlands, N.J.: Humanities Press, 1982), p. 217.

23 Marjorie Perloff, 'The Two *Ariels* . . .' in Fraistat (ed.), *Poems in their Place*. And the American poet Dave Smith maintains 'It is a perverse logic which begins with the fact of Plath's suicide and works back to find the poems as scripts of illness. Poetry kept Sylvia Plath alive . . .'; see 'Sylvia Plath, the Electric Horse' in Wagner (ed.), *Sylvia Plath*, p. 275.

24 Lowell in an interview with Frederick Seidel, *Collected Prose*, pp. 246–7. See also Eileen Aird's gloss on this remark with regard to the bee poems, in her essay on Plath's poetic development in Wagner (ed.), *Sylvia Plath*, p. 196.

Chapter 7 – Speaking as a Woman

1 Helen Vendler, 'Sylvia Plath', *Part of Nature, Part of Us: modern American poets* (Cambridge, Massachusetts and London: Harvard

University Press, 1980), p. 271. See also Hughes's remark that all Plath's early poems are evidence to some extent of her divided self: 'the opposition of a prickly, fastidious defence and an imminent volcano' ('Notes on the Chronological Order . . .', p. 188).

2 The lines seem to look forward to the poem of burial instructions, 'Last Words' (p. 172):

> I do not trust the spirit. It escapes like steam
> In dreams, through mouth-hole or eye-hole. I can't stop it.
> One day it won't come back.

and the second voice in *Three Women*:

> I hold my fingers up, ten white pickets.
> See, the darkness is leaking from the cracks.
> I cannot contain it. I cannot contain my life.

See Steven Gould Axelrod, *Sylvia Plath* pp. 205 ff, where he relates this idea of a vanishing soul to Plath's reading for her undergraduate thesis, especially of James Frazer's *Golden Bough*. Her thesis, 'The Magic Mirror', concerned the theme of the double in two of Dostoevsky's novels.

3 The ambiguity of the ending is similar to that in 'Tulips' (p. 160), a poem that repays careful reading.

4 These figures are taken from C.S. Butler's Chatterton lecture, 'Poetry and the Computer: some quantitative aspects of the style of Sylvia Plath' in the *Proceedings of the British Academy 1979*, vol. LXV (London: Oxford University Press, 1981). He points out that the one unexpected result from his research is the frequency of possessives and contractions, a feature of informal speech which nevertheless is more present in *The Colossus* than in *Ariel*.

5 Lowell, *Collected Prose*, p. 227.

6 Helen McNeil, 'Sylvia Plath' in Helen Vendler (ed.), *Voices and Visions: the Poet in America* (New York: Random House, 1987), p. 471.

7 Calvin Bedient suggests that the tragedy of Plath's life is not a tragedy of will, as in classical drama, but of weakness, 'a fatal vulnerability to the sense of injury'. 'It looks like a senseless failure, but it has a romantic power.' 'Sylvia Plath, Romantic . . .' in Gary Lane (ed.), *Sylvia Plath: new views on the poetry* (Baltimore and London: Johns Hopkins University Press, 1979).

8 Stan Smith, 'Waist-deep in History', p. 221.

9 Sandra M. Gilbert, 'A Fine White Flying Myth' in Gilbert and Gubar (eds), *Shakespeare's Sisters*, p. 247.

10 Barbara Hardy, 'The Poetry of Sylvia Plath' in Sue Roe (ed.), *Women Reading Women's Writing* (Brighton: Harvester Press, 1987), pp. 215, 218.

11 'Words' has been analysed by Steven Gould Axelrod in terms of Plath's use of texts by male poets as part of her argument with their tradition. In particular, he points to the way its last lines remind us of Gloucester's words in *King Lear*, and uses this to discuss Plath's relationship to Shakespeare as an authority to be admired but also resented. See his *Sylvia Plath*, pp. 74–9.

12 'Context' in *Johnny Panic*, pp. 92–3. The examples Plath gives are 'certain poems in Robert Lowell's *Life Studies*, for instance; Theodore Roethke's greenhouse poems; some of Elizabeth Bishop and a very great deal of Stevie Smith ("Art is wild as a cat and quite separate from civilization")'.

13 Hughes, 'Notes on the Chronological Order of Sylvia Plath's Poems', p. 187.

14 Stephen Spender's review of *Ariel* in *New Republic* (June 1966), reprinted in Linda W. Wagner (ed.), *Sylvia Plath*, p. 72. Mary Ellmann has characteristically dry remarks to make about the male use of the word 'hysteria' with reference to this review and to Plath in *Thinking About Women*, pp. 82–7. Her other references to Plath in the book are equally interesting, in the context of reflections on female stereotypes in the work of male writers and reviewers.

15 Hugh Kenner, 'The Plath Celebration: a partial dissent' (1973), reprinted in Harold Bloom (ed.), *Sylvia Plath* (New York and Philadelphia: Chelsea House, 1989), pp. 14–15.

16 Franz Kafka, letter to Oskar Pollak, 27 January 1904, in *Letters to Friends, Family and Editors*, trans. Richard and Clara Winston (New York: Schocken Books, 1977), p. 16. Anne Sexton used the lines about the book as axe as epigraph for her collection *All My Pretty Ones* (1962). See also Plath's protest to her mother against writing 'cheerful stuff', *Letters Home*, p. 473.

Suggestions for Further Reading

Works by Sylvia Plath

The Colossus. London: Heinemann, 1960.

The Bell Jar. London: Heinemann, 1963 (published under the pseudonym Victoria Lucas); republished, Faber & Faber, 1963.

Ariel. London: Faber & Faber, 1965.

Crossing the Water. London: Faber & Faber, 1971.

Winter Trees. London: Faber & Faber, 1971.

Letters Home: Correspondence 1950–1963. Ed. with commentary by Aurelia Schober Plath. London: Faber & Faber, 1975.

The Bed Book. London: Faber & Faber, 1976.

Johnny Panic and the Bible of Dreams. London: Faber & Faber 1977; 1979.

The Collected Poems. Ed. Ted Hughes. London: Faber & Faber, 1981.

The Journals of Sylvia Plath. Ed. Frances McCullough; consulting ed. Ted Hughes. New York: Dial Press, 1982.

The Colossus and *The Bell Jar* were the only books by Plath to be published in her lifetime; all her posthumous publications (differing versions being issued in the United Kingdom and the United States) have been edited by Ted Hughes. Various collections were re-grouped in chronological order for the *Collected Poems*; this does not include her rhyming catalogue of desirable beds, *The Bed Book*, a children's poem published separately in 1976. *Johnny Panic* has a longer introduction in its first edition than in the later paperback. *Letters Home* is a doubly edited version of the life – what a daughter chooses to tell her mother, what the mother elects to publish – but a valuable compilation, with good photographs.

For further biographical material, it is worth consulting Nancy Hunter Steiner's *A Closer Look at Ariel: a Memory of Sylvia Plath* (London: Faber & Faber, 1974), which covers the Cambridge period; Edward Butscher (ed.), *Sylvia Plath: the Woman and the Work* (London: Peter Owen, 1979) includes memoirs by friends as well as essays on the poetry. Of the two major biographies, Linda Wagner-Martin's *Sylvia Plath* (London: Chatto & Windus, 1988) is the more sympathetic to her subject; Anne Stevenson's *Bitter Fame* (London: Viking, 1989) has been passed by Hughes as accurate, but has been very controversial because of its presentation of 'the case against Plath' – see, for example, the cross-fire in *Poetry Review* (79:4; 80:1; 80:3). Both biographies are now available in paperback editions. Ronald Hayman's *The Death and Life of Sylvia Plath* (London: Heinemann, 1991) has just been published: the title set off warning bells, and I would not recommend it.

Two books that I have found particularly helpful in putting Plath's work in context are Eric Homberger's *The Art of the Real* (London: J.M. Dent, 1977), which parallels the development of British and American poetry from 1939 to the mid-1970s, and Richard Gray's *American Poetry of the Twentieth Century* (London & New York: Longman, 1990), which deftly sketches in the political and cultural background, and provides good bibliographies. Useful anthologies of poetry by Plath's contemporaries, besides Alvarez's *The New Poetry* (Harmondsworth: Penguin, 1962, revised 1966), include Donald Hall's *Contemporary American Poetry* (Harmondsworth: Penguin, 1962, revised 1972); and for a wider view, Geoffrey Moore (ed.), *The Penguin Book of American Verse* (1977), and *The Faber Book of Twentieth Century Women's Poetry* (1987), edited by Fleur Adcock, who maintains that the four outstanding women poets of the century are Marianne Moore, Elizabeth Bishop, Stevie Smith and Sylvia Plath (she rejects Anne Sexton as 'excessively derivative').

The number of books and articles devoted to Plath's work since the 1970s is dauntingly large, and by no means all are worthwhile. A comprehensive listing of those up to 1985 may be found in Stephen Tabor, *Sylvia Plath: an Analytic Bibliography* (London and New York: Mansell, 1986). There are several collections of essays offering a cross-section of opinions on Plath's achievements: Charles Newman (ed.), *The Art of Sylvia Plath* (London: Faber & Faber, 1970) includes pieces by Hughes, Anne Sexton and reprints Steiner's chapter from *Language and Silence*; from Gary Lane (ed.), *Sylvia Plath: New Views on the Poetry* (Baltimore and London: Johns Hopkins University Press, 1979), I recommend the essay by Bedient on Plath as a 'romantic', J.D. McClatchy's overview of her work, and Carole Ferrier on the beekeeping poems; see also Paul Alexander (ed.), *Ariel Ascending: Writings about Sylvia Plath* (New York: Harper & Row, 1985). Linda Wagner-Martin's volume for the critical heritage series, *Sylvia Plath* (London: Routledge, 1988) provides a selection of contemporary as well as posthumous reviews of the poetry and prose.

I have mentioned in the notes Susan Bassnett's recent, brief study *Sylvia Plath* (London: Macmillan, 1987), which perhaps leans over backwards to make Plath into a less complicated poet and person than I believe her to have been; Axelrod's *Sylvia Plath: the wound and the cure of words* (Baltimore and London: Johns Hopkins University Press, 1990) works in the other direction. A balanced assessment of the poetry is provided by Eileen Aird's short book, *Sylvia Plath: Her Life and Work* (Edinburgh: Oliver & Boyd, 1973); see also Mary Lynn Broe, *Protean Poetic: the Poetry of Sylvia Plath* (Columbia: University of Missouri Press, 1980); Jon Rosenblatt, *Sylvia Plath: the Poetry of Initiation* (Chapel Hill: University of North Carolina Press, 1979) and Margaret Dickie Uroff, *Sylvia Plath and Ted Hughes* (Urbana: University of Illinois

Press, 1979). Jacqueline Rose's thesis, in *The Haunting of Sylvia Plath* (London: Virago, 1991), is that Plath 'writes at the point of tension – pleasure/danger, your fault/my fault, high/low culture – without resolution or dissipation of what produces the clash between the two'; her study avoids imposing an artificial consistency on the woman or her work, and discusses what both have meant to subsequent generations.

Besides the essays (mentioned in footnotes above) by Barbara Hardy, Helen McNeil, Stan Smith and Helen Vendler, which provide some of the best Plath criticism, there are a couple of others that I should like to recommend: Alan Williamson's chapter on Plath in his *Introspection and Contemporary Poetry* (Cambridge, Massachusetts: Harvard University Press, 1984), as well as his general chapter on 'Personal Poetry'; and the sophisticated exploration of Plath's language by Mutlu Kornuk Blasing, Chapter 3 of *American Poetry: the Rhetoric of its Forms* (New Haven: Yale University Press, 1987). For *The Bell Jar*, see Tony Tanner's chapter on the novel in his study of American fiction in the period 1950–1970, *City of Words* (London: Jonathan Cape, 1971).

Plath's work is rich terrain for feminist literary criticism: see Toril Moi's *Sexual/Textual Politics* (London: Routledge, 1985) for an excellent guide to feminist literary theory; it also has a comprehensive bibliography. Alice Ostriker's *Stealing the Language* (London: The Women's Press, 1987) is valuable for its wide-ranging discussion of women's poetry in America – the chapters on body language and on anger are particularly relevant to Plath, but she is referred to throughout. Ostriker also has a powerful essay on Plath's language, 'The Americanization of Sylvia', in her collection *Writing Like a Woman* (Ann Arbor: The University of Michigan Press, 1983). In addition to the essay footnoted above (ch. 3 n. 2), Sandra M. Gilbert interestingly compares Plath's *Three Women* with Woolf's *The Waves* in 'In Yeats's House: the Death and Resurrection of Sylvia Plath' in Diane Wood Middlebrook and Marilyn Yalom (eds), *Coming to Light: American women poets in the twentieth century* (Ann Arbor: University of Michigan Press, 1983).

And if you are tired of all these conflicting voices, you may like to find Plath's own: Hardwick describes her reading as 'full-throated, plump, diction-perfect, Englishy, mesmerizing cadences, all round and rapid, and paced and spaced'. Plath reads 'Lady Lazarus', 'Daddy' and 'Fever 103°' on *The Poet Speaks: 5 – Ted Hughes, Peter Porter, Thom Gunn, Sylvia Plath* (London: Argo Record Co., 1965).

Index